STAR WARS®

ATTACK OF THE CLONES™
THE VISUAL DICTIONARY

KYD-21
blaster

Comlink
system

Mabari emblem
cape seal

Wrist-guard
gauntlet

Breathpack

Elastic bodysuit
accommodates
shape-shifting

Blast-energy
sink skirt

Shin-guard
boots

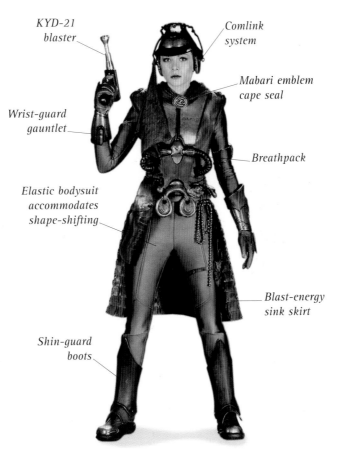

ZAM WESELL

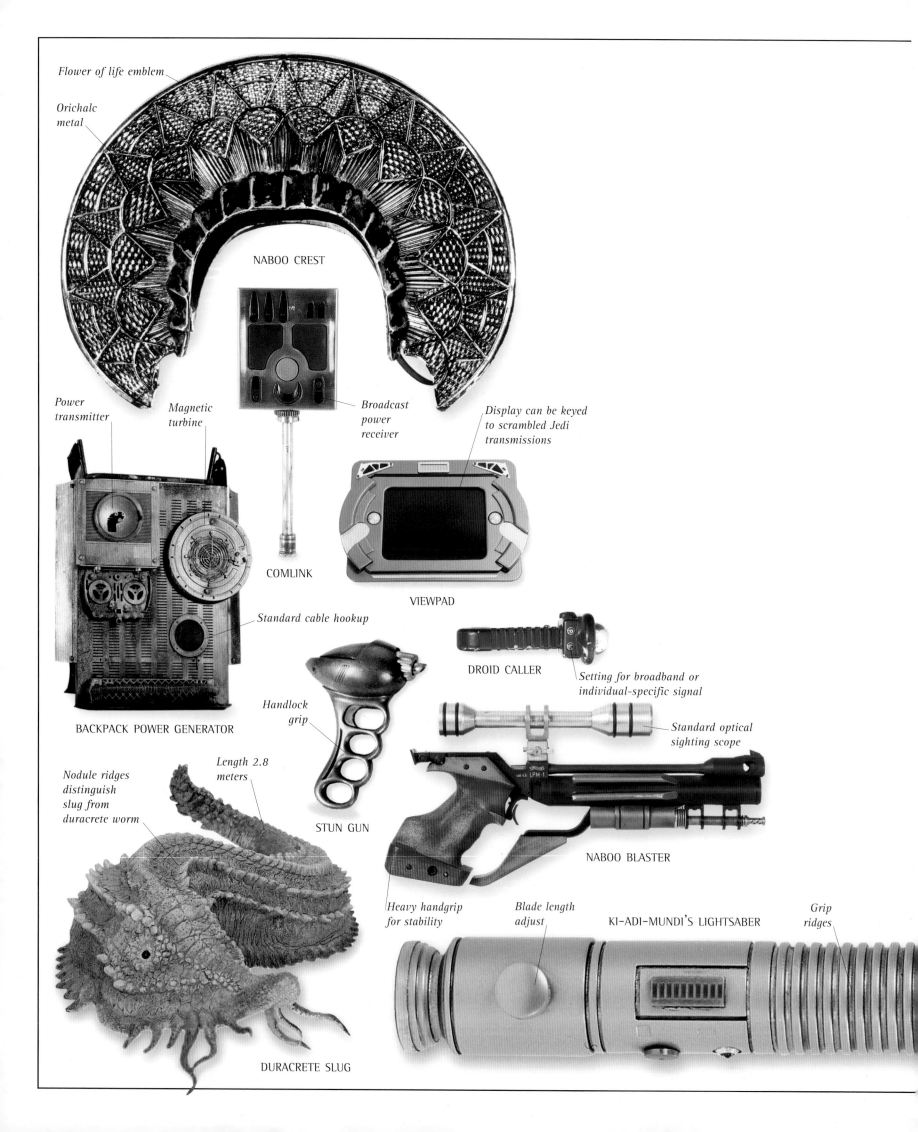

Flower of life emblem

Orichalc metal

NABOO CREST

Power transmitter

Magnetic turbine

Broadcast power receiver

Display can be keyed to scrambled Jedi transmissions

COMLINK

VIEWPAD

Standard cable hookup

BACKPACK POWER GENERATOR

DROID CALLER

Setting for broadband or individual-specific signal

Handlock grip

Standard optical sighting scope

Nodule ridges distinguish slug from duracrete worm

Length 2.8 meters

STUN GUN

NABOO BLASTER

Heavy handgrip for stability

Blade length adjust

KI-ADI-MUNDI'S LIGHTSABER

Grip ridges

DURACRETE SLUG

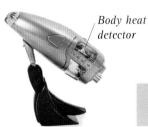

Body heat detector

SECURITY MONITOR

Ancient demagogue

SISTROS STATUE

STAR WARS

ATTACK OF THE CLONES™
THE VISUAL DICTIONARY

Written by DAVID WEST REYNOLDS

Special fabrications by ROBERT E. BARNES, DON BIES, & JOHN GOODSON
New photography by ALEX IVANOV

Action bodysuit

Jedi tunic

Parry 4 position

Attack 5 position

Synthetic leather surcoat

Reversed attack stance

DEFENDERS OF JUSTICE

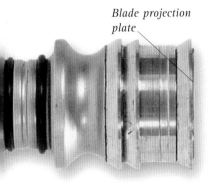

Blade projection plate

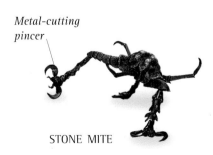

Metal-cutting pincer

STONE MITE

www.starwars.com www.dk.com

Contents

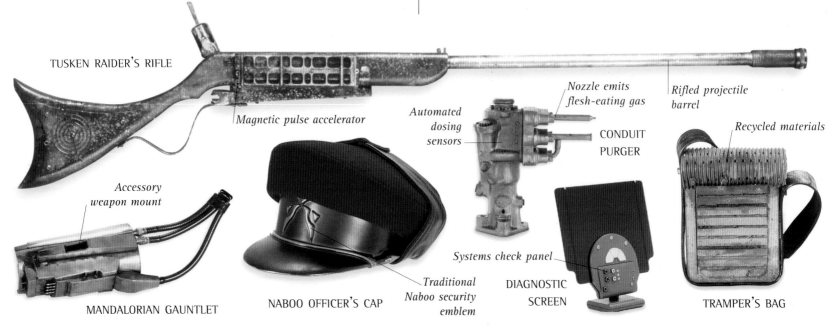

TUSKEN RAIDER'S RIFLE

Magnetic pulse accelerator

Nozzle emits flesh-eating gas

Rifled projectile barrel

Automated dosing sensors

CONDUIT PURGER

Recycled materials

Accessory weapon mount

Systems check panel

Traditional Naboo security emblem

DIAGNOSTIC SCREEN

MANDALORIAN GAUNTLET

NABOO OFFICER'S CAP

TRAMPER'S BAG

Introduction

IN A TIME OF INSTABILITY, the galaxy stands on the brink of rupture as powerful forces threaten to tear the Republic apart. The small numbers of peacekeeping Jedi cannot quell outright rebellion, and the great commercial powers are increasingly lured by the temptations of greed. Disruptive changes are at hand and the lines between good and evil are becoming unclear. Amid these epochal events, the galaxy's fate will turn upon the choices of only a few individuals, whose destinies are clouded. The Jedi have already lost a great leader with the defection of Count Dooku—will they now be forced to engage in the first full-scale war since the inception of the Republic? Where lies the path of honor in this uncertain time? When the valiant must choose between love and duty, peace and war, danger waits in every breath.

Trace in these pages the faces of legend, the shadows of inner turmoil, and the instruments of fate as one by one the final elements of a terrible destiny unfold.

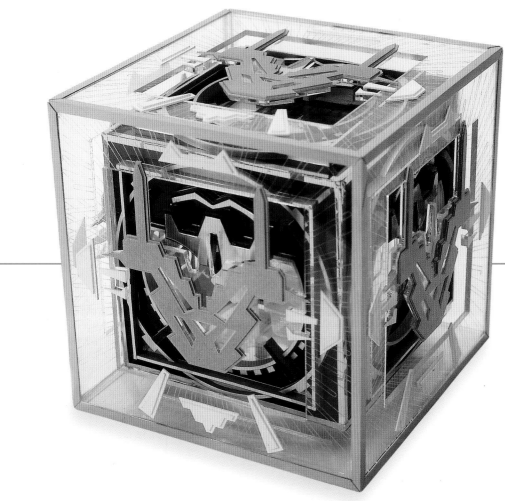

JEDI HOLOCRON

The Growing Darkness

LONG AGO, a prophesy foretold the coming of an individual who would "bring balance to the Force," ushering in a new era of peace following one of great instability. With the Separatist crisis, the future of the great Galactic Republic is clouded with uncertainty and the peace-keeping Jedi are too few to hold together an entire galaxy. In this age, the Sith have reappeared, their evil hidden perhaps in the heart of liberty's citadel—and while the prophecy is looked upon anew, many of the galaxy's denizens have no choice but to fend for themselves.

Beyond the vision of the Jedi Knights, somewhere within the darkness, the greatest master of evil ever to use Sith power bides his time. As his strength grows, his plans begin to shape the course of the galaxy, and his snares await the unsuspecting.

A Time of Change

Below the spires of Coruscant where the Jedi High Council and the Senate debate how to resolve the Separatist crisis, ordinary people struggle through a period of growing unrest. Ancient patterns are in upheaval and vast populations are on the move. In such a time, individuals must learn self-reliance and trust in what they can carry.

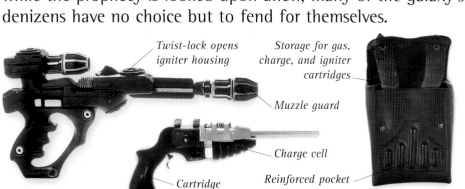

Twist-lock opens igniter housing

Storage for gas, charge, and igniter cartridges

Muzzle guard

Charge cell

Cartridge housing

Reinforced pocket

BLASTERS

PROBES

Pack holds samples of hot volcanic ore

CARTRIDGE POUCH

Reinforced covering

MESH GLOVES

Enhanced parallax sensors

Holographic display

Accessory mount plate

Module holds scouting information

Display screen

Melt-proof Ceramoid mesh

SCANNER

Anti-microbe field plate

Antithermic frame

Demagnetizing terminal

RECORD PAD

Discharge trigger

SURVIVAL OXYGEN

Zoom dial

Anti-static tube

Universal weatherproof housing

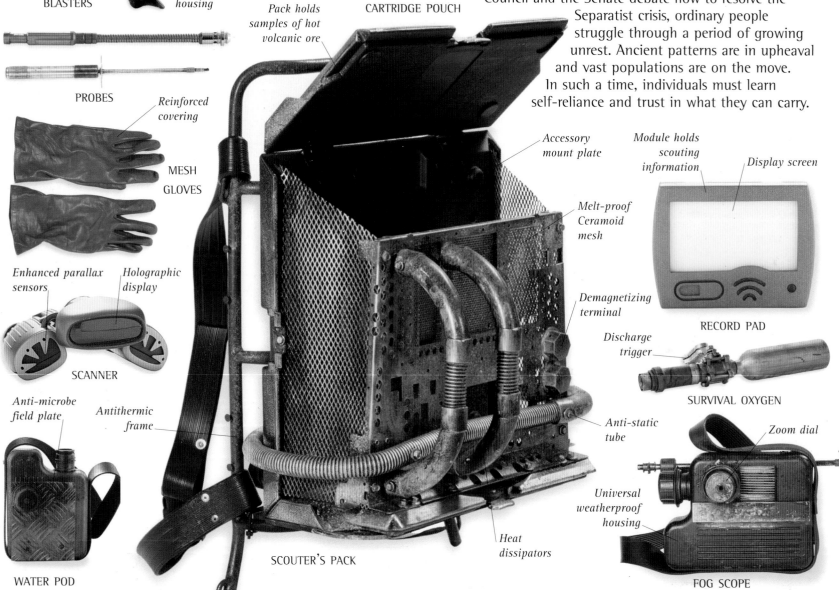

WATER POD

SCOUTER'S PACK

Heat dissipators

FOG SCOPE

Jedi Padawan learner's braid reveals true identity to a Jedi initiate

Thousand Moons young matron's dress

Pattern common in Thousand Moons system

Private spire of Raith Seinar, military spacecraft engineering genius

Hidden Demons

Anakin Skywalker's fate has made him a Jedi and brought him to the center of events at the galactic capital. Senior Council members suspect he is the Chosen One. But like Coruscant itself, Anakin contends with inner demons against which an ancient prophecy seems little help.

Squad of clone troopers

Since its inception, the Republic has been protected by its system of law rather than by the force of armies. But the law is only as strong as its people, and when their vigilance fades, armies may regain the upper hand.

Jedi boots in altered color

DATA FILE

◆ Many Coruscant freighters designed for hauling cargo are now forced by necessity to carry many hundreds of passengers as well.

◆ Military expenditures in the Republic are dramatically rising during this troubled period.

Refugees

Anakin Skywalker and the woman he is protecting flee Coruscant in disguise, but they cannot hide from the Sith. In the time of greatest crisis, they are caught within the plans of the powerful, and like all galactic refugees, find they must rely on their inner resources.

Severe hairstyle conforms to diplomatic etiquette

Neckband is gift from Naboo Council

Senator Padmé Amidala

As ELECTED QUEEN of Naboo, Padmé Amidala won the lasting devotion of her people by showing extraordinary strength of character during the Trade Federation invasion. On the expiration of her second and final term of office, she yielded her authority in spite of popular demand for a change in the law that would have allowed her to rule longer. She was soon elected Senator to represent the 36 Naboo regional star systems; Padmé now travels widely to build support for her causes, returning to the galactic capital of Coruscant when necessary.

Senator Amidala's retinue returns to Coruscant in the sleek Naboo Cruiser to speak against a vote on the Military Creation Act. Padmé lands amidst high tensions and an invisible web of intrigue.

Cordé (disguised as Padmé)

Dormé

Like the Naboo Queen, Padmé is served and protected in vulnerable situations by loyal handmaidens who can act as decoys, assuming Padmé's identity, appearance, and dress.

Streamlined body for easy deployment from within garments

Naboo chrome finish

BLASTER

New tactical pilot suit

N-1 Camouflage

For security, Padmé sometimes travels disguised as a Naboo starfighter pilot. Other planetary Senators would never condescend to yield the trappings of their status, so the simple ruse is effective.

Senatorial gown more low-key and practical than royal display garments Padmé wore as Queen

Auto-encrypting comm unit

Starfighter pilot emblem

Anti-glare goggles

Supplementary oxygen hookup

STARFIGHTER HELMET

Senatorial Dress

Padmé dresses with decorum when speaking in the Senate on important issues. A tireless champion of peace and freedom, she has worked for years against a much-debated proposal to create a great army of the Republic, which she believes might be the catalyst for war.

Senatorial Accomodation

While on Coruscant, Padmé and her retinue reside in quarters atop one of the ancient skyscrapers. Living in anything less than a penthouse would diminish Padmé's standing on the status-obsessed world and impede her diplomatic efforts. While the quarters are comfortable, Padmé loathes Coruscant's gray, artificial environment.

Padmé's apartment

Padmé's modest rooms do not have the fortress-like security systems used by more sophisticated politicians. The Senator sleeps exposed to many unseen dangers.

UNTIMELY RETREAT

It takes two assassination attempts to convince Padmé to leave Coruscant for the safety of Naboo. Her retreat is a bitter one, for she will likely be absent during the vote on the army proposal and flight is alien to her character.

Subdued colors express grave mood

Synthetic leather gauntlets for hand-to-hand combat

Naboo blaster

Captain Typho oversees security for Senator Amidala and her retinue. He is the nephew of Captain Panaka, who served Padmé while she was Queen of Naboo.

Corset of light armor that doubles as protection

Captain Typho

Raised to his Senatorial post because of his uncompromising loyalty and his ties to Panaka, Captain Typho is a relative novice to the world of lethal subterfuge that most galactic representatives in the Senate take for granted.

Traditional security tunic

Fabric hides uncomfortable blast-damping underskirt

DATA FILE

◆ Naboo soldiers compose most of Captain Typho's security force on Coruscant.

◆ Captain Typho's eye patch is a mark of dedication, since he lost his eye in the line of duty.

Naboo military boots

Positive traction grip soles

Supreme Chancellor Palpatine

PALPATINE IS CAREFUL TO present himself as a mild-mannered servant of the public good, avoiding ostentation and ever protesting the limits of his abilities. Palpatine ascended to office amid mass frustration with the previous Supreme Chancellor—but there is increasing evidence that Palpatine himself quietly built much of this opinion behind the scenes. It also seems that a pattern may be emerging in Palpatine's work as Supreme Chancellor: Always citing the best interests of the Republic, he has consistently increased his own power, from legal authority to his institution of the Chancellor's Red Guard, who now attend every committee meeting. For some, his true intentions remain unclear.

Sleeves of ancient design

Subdued color and simple style convey gravity without pompous exhibitionism

Security Innovator

The Supreme Chancellor has placed the new Red Guard under his direct authority, while a Senatorial committee oversees the old Blue Guard. Palpatine calls this an efficient streamlining of cumbersome bureaucracy. Objectors have called it an illegal personal bodyguard, but such talk runs the risk of violating Palpatine's new security laws.

Although he prefers to avoid ostentation, Palpatine heeds the tradition for high political officials to maintain impressive audience chambers. During meetings, the large, scenic window reminds those involved that their decisions have wide repercussions.

Face shield protects Red Guard's identity

Blue Guard

Red Guard summoner

Ultra-dense lanthanide alloy armor

Red Guard force pike

Hidden shield generator

Blue Guard rifle

SEAT OF OFFICE
Palpatine has bowed to the concerns of his aides by accepting a special chair of office that affords him secret shielding and cunning protection. This chair also provides direct, secure communication with Palpatine's aides and with the Red Guard.

Ceremonial stylings

The Red Guard

Palpatine has kept the details of the Red Guard's training secret, citing security concerns. No one seems to know where this protection force and its trappings come from. Instead of stun rifles, the Red Guard use force pikes, which are more likely to be lethal.

Eyes see only in
ultraviolet light

Umbaran
shadowcloak
is patterned
in ultraviolet
colors

Attack and
display
horns

Lethorns

The Jedi Council often discusses political opinions with Supreme
Chancellor Palpatine. The support of the great Jedi reassures many
who might otherwise doubt the Chancellor's motives.

Sly Moore and Mas Amedda

Sly Moore is Palpatine's Staff Aide. She controls access to the
Chancellor, which gives her tremendous power. Moore comes
from the shadowy world of Umbara, deep within the dark
reaches of the Ghost Nebula. Umbarans are known for their
abilities to subtly influence, and even control, others.
As Speaker of the Senate, Mas Amedda is responsible for
keeping order in debates. He is a stern and stoic Chagrian,
who refuses to
comment on
the changes he
has witnessed
during
Palpatine's
tenure.

While the average citizen has grown weary of politics,
momentous events are afoot. Separatists foment unrest, and
rumors are rife of secret armies. In ages past, safeguards
limited the power of the Supreme Chancellor—but
Palpatine calls them impediments
to effective leadership,
and may soon
overturn them, with
substantial support.

OFFICE IDOLS
Palpatine's statues
honor obscure figures
from the past who
possessed much arcane
wisdom and law, but
whose actions are
shrouded in
controversy.

DATA FILE

◆ Palpatine's term ended several years ago,
but a series of crises has allowed him to stay
in office beyond the Senate's legal limit.

◆ Close aides say that Palpatine sometimes
works for days without sleeping.

◆ Palpatine has revived the old tradition of
appearing before the masses to accept their
applause and vocal support.

The Senate

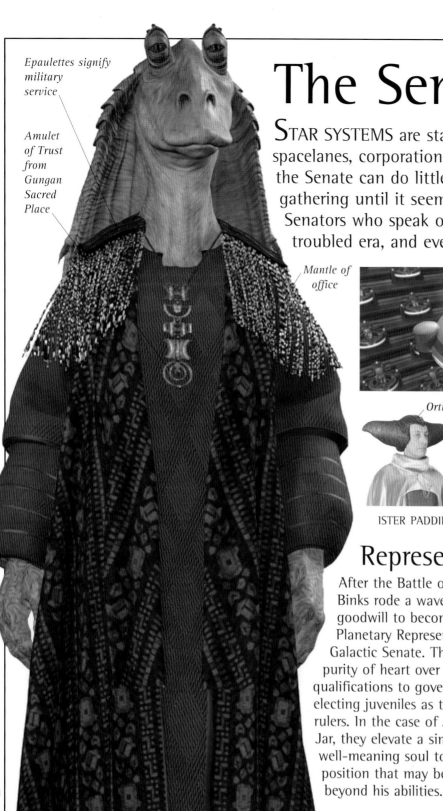

Epaulettes signify military service

Amulet of Trust from Gungan Sacred Place

STAR SYSTEMS are starving under heavy taxation. Pirates plague the spacelanes, corporations consume worlds, bureaucracy stifles justice—and yet the Senate can do little. Power and wealth are corrupting this once-noble gathering until it seems that soon only money will have a voice. Honest Senators who speak out are becoming rare. Few leaders light the way in this troubled era, and even the Jedi are beginning to be unsure whom to trust.

Mantle of office

In Padmé's absence, Jar Jar represents Naboo in the Senate. With the best of intentions, Jar Jar sets in motion a new galactic era as he proposes a motion for the Supreme Chancellor to accept emergency powers.

Orthodox Halbara hairstyle

Sybarion gown

ISTER PADDIE   **LEXI DIO**   **SUPI**

Some Senators adopt the fashions of Coruscant, while others maintain the traditions of their homeworlds. Senators' clothing, styling, and mode of conduct can offer clues to their political sympathies.

Representative Binks

After the Battle of Naboo, Jar Jar Binks rode a wave of Naboo goodwill to become Associate Planetary Representative in the Galactic Senate. The Naboo value purity of heart over other qualifications to govern, often electing juveniles as their rulers. In the case of Jar Jar, they elevate a simple, well-meaning soul to a position that may be beyond his abilities.

Traditional banner

Few Senators can completely resist the temptation to indulge themselves. Nations, worlds, systems, and staggering wealth can be had in illicit exchange for votes or strategic abstentions on critical legislation.

DATA FILE

◆ The motion for emergency dictatorial powers—the Military Creation Act—is one of the few proposals that demand an immediate vote by the Senate.

◆ The Anx Senators are among the small number who openly support Bail Organa's uncompromising moral code.

Bail Organa

Bail Organa of Alderaan is a noble Senator in an ignoble time. In ages past, he would have been revered as a great leader. Amid the current moral decay, Bail's colleagues demean him as simplistic for his eloquent and impassioned support of the value of civic virtue.

Alderaanian patrician boots

Droids

DROIDS RANGE FROM simple machines to complex, sentient artificial beings. They are generally treated as mere utility devices regardless of their level of intelligence, and most citizens hardly notice them. Memory wipes, which are customarily performed when a droid acquires a new owner, can delete filed information or completely erase a droid's stored experiences. When "zeroed" this way, even sophisticated droids may be rendered barely self-aware. If allowed to build experience between memory wipes, some droids seem to develop individual identities and even idiosyncratic personalities.

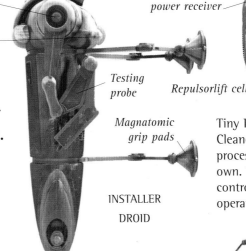

Probe servo

Signal receiver

Testing probe

Repulsorlift cell

Magnatomic grip pads

INSTALLER DROID

Broadcast signal and power receiver

Electrostatic polisher

CLEANER DROID

Tiny Installer Droids and Cleaner Droids have no processor power of their own. They are tied to master control systems that broadcast operating commands.

Added memory housing

Tools behind panels

Standardized body

Treaded drives

Retractable third leg

Location transmitter

Retrieval signal receptor

Vocoder

Audio pickup

Processor housing

Extensible neck

Heavy casing

Astromech Droids

"Astro Droids" are multipurpose computer repair and information retrieval systems. They are given just enough processor power to do their jobs, communicating only via electronic beeps and whistles. Astro Droids have an inclination to exceed their programming if their stored experiences develop far enough.

Light-duty manipulator arm

Balance gyro

Low-dexterity graspers

Drive wheel

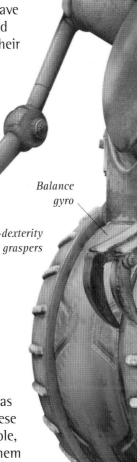

DATA FILE

◆ Droids are frequently misused because galactic law treats them as machinery regardless of their self-awareness.

◆ Droids are banned on some worlds where their ultrasonic frequencies irritate sensitive species.

On Tatooine, Unipod Droids pull rickshaws that float on unlicensed broadcast-power repulsors.

Unipod Droid

Compact, semi-humanoid Unipod Droids are an ancient model that has seen little change for centuries. These stoutly built droids are highly reliable, but their minimal processors suit them for little more than simple manual labor.

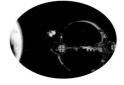

HYPERDRIVE RING

Obi-Wan Kenobi

A DEDICATED JEDI KNIGHT facing a time of great crisis, Obi-Wan Kenobi finds himself at the heart of galactic turmoil as the Republic begins to unravel. Kenobi has witnessed the death of his Master, Qui-Gon Jinn, and knows the challenges the Jedi face in the defense of justice. He is cautious where his apprentice, Anakin Skywalker, is impulsive. Kenobi strives to train his young Padawan in the discipline that will make him a pillar of strength against the dark side of the Force. As dangers unfold around him, Kenobi's abilities and judgment form one of the last bulwarks against the collapse of the Republic.

SCANNER   COMLINK

Traditional leather utility belt

Lightsaber

Obi-Wan's Jedi apprentice is Anakin Skywalker, the boy suspected of being the prophesied individual who can "bring balance to the Force." Anakin's independence, born of his late induction into the Order, has brought Kenobi reprimands from Jedi elders Yoda and Mace Windu.

Trailing a would-be assassin into a nightclub on Coruscant, Kenobi steps casually to the bar "to have a drink." As planned, his apparent relaxation draws out his quarry, who finds that the Jedi's extraordinary powers give him a lightning edge—it is virtually impossible to take Obi-Wan by surprise.

Utility pouch

Food and energy capsules

Jedi tunic layered to adapt to different environments

Jedi robe

Rugged travel boots

DATA FILE

◆ The quartermasters in the Jedi Temple issue Obi-Wan with field equipment, such as this scanner monitor.

◆ Obi-Wan focused on Form III lightsaber training after the death of Qui-Gon Jinn.

Long hair of Jedi Knight

Two-handed grip for full saber control

Blade emitter

Blade modulation circuitry

Blade length and intensity control

Activator

Blade power adjust

Internal blade crystals

Handgrip

Power cell housing

Form III brace-ready stance

Kenobi specializes in Form III lightsaber combat, which maximizes defensive protection. Invented ages ago when blaster weapons first became common in the hands of Jedi enemies, Form III began as high-speed laserblast deflection training. Over the centuries, it has been refined into an expression of nonaggressive Jedi philosophy.

Piloting a Delta-7 starfighter on his field mission, Obi-Wan relies on a built-in Astromech Droid called R4-P17 to manage shipboard systems independently.

Captured on Geonosis, Kenobi comes face-to-face with Count Dooku, who once trained Qui-Gon Jinn. The Count tempts Obi-Wan with an offer of power in the Separatist regime, but Kenobi's dedication to justice is incorruptible.

Field Agent

Accomplished in a wide variety of skills ranging from diplomacy and psychology to military strategy and hand-to-hand combat, Obi-Wan has to be ready for anything on his field assignments. On Kamino, his investigation bursts into explosive conflict when bounty hunter Jango Fett resists arrest. Covered in armor and weaponry, Fett is a professional at the top of his field, but he cannot overcome Obi-Wan. The best Fett can manage is escape—with a powerful tracer beacon attached to his ship.

Signal port

TRACER BEACON

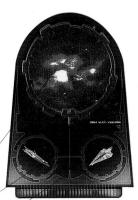

Star Tracker

Pursuing Jango Fett across the galaxy, Obi-Wan engages in a space duel with Fett and his deadly spacecraft, *Slave I*. Obi-Wan proves his abilities as an expert pilot and tactician, sacrificing his spare parts in a ruse to put Fett off his trail with apparent explosion debris. From high in orbit, Obi-Wan's top-of-the-line starfighter sensor suite then traces Fett down to the weird planet surface of Geonosis.

Wide-band sensor scan

Sensor select monitor

Systems impedance monitor

STARFIGHTER DISPLAYS

Graphic damage monitor

Facing off against Count Dooku, Kenobi wisely exercises restraint where his apprentice rushes in headlong. A Jedi of powerful inner focus, Obi-Wan nevertheless finds he is unprepared for the Count's specialist techniques. Against Kenobi's Form III moves, the Count demonstrates the ancient and elegant precision of Form II lightsaber combat.

Anakin Skywalker

TWENTY-YEAR-OLD Jedi Padawan Anakin Skywalker is gifted with extraordinary Force skills and piloting abilities. His talents make him impatient with Jedi traditions that seem to hold him back and he often disagrees with his more cautious Jedi Master, Obi-Wan Kenobi. Skywalker was accepted into the Order at the age of ten, far later in life than its rules allow, and his emotional bond with his mother was already strong. Unlike other Jedi, Anakin struggles with the pain of this separation. Jedi Council members suspect Anakin of being the prophesied One who can bring balance to the Force. But in an increasingly unbalanced world, Anakin must face ever steeper challenges to master the dangerous force that is himself.

Padawan's short hairstyle with learner braid

Standard Jedi tunic

Synthetic leather surcoat offers more protection than traditional cloth garment

Anakin is capable but not yet professional, criticizing his Master Kenobi in front of their charge, Senator Amidala. Anakin prefers to exceed his and Obi-Wan's mandate to only protect Padmé by trying to discover who is after her.

Comlink pouch

Medical kit

Mechanical tool pouch

Food and energy capsules

LIGHTSABER

UTILITY BELT

Unconventional tunic color expresses Anakin's independence

Most Jedi Padawans build their lightsabers to resemble those of their Masters as a gesture of respect. Anakin constructed his own lightsaber while in a trance-like state, resulting in a design that favors maximum strength.

Blue lightsaber blade generated via traditional Jedi crystals is more maneuverable but slightly less powerful than blade using synthetic Sith crystals

Heavy duty body cylinder

Activator and power indicator

Power-cell housing

Dark Knight

The tunics, robes, and cloaks worn by Jedi are honored traditions, but not uniforms. From the time they become Padawans, Jedi are free to dress as they choose. Anakin Skywalker breaks with tradition in his garments, both in their color and material. His distinctive dark clothing makes him stand out at the Jedi Temple and draws concern from Jedi elders.

Synthetic leather protective boots

Field boots weighted for training

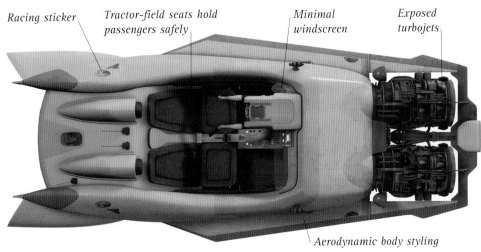

Racing sticker

Tractor-field seats hold passengers safely

Minimal windscreen

Exposed turbojets

Aerodynamic body styling

Airspeed

Anakin is possibly the best pilot ever to train within the Jedi Temple. When he commandeers an airspeeder in pursuit of an assassin on Coruscant, his abilities are phenomenal. Anakin violates Jedi policies on vehicular speed and risk—guidelines intended to safeguard other craft, but not designed with so gifted a pilot in mind. Anakin's antics prompt the remark from Obi Wan, "Why do I get the feeling you're going to be the death of me?"

Headdress disguise for Padmé

Forbidden Feelings

Only 20 Jedi have ever left the Order, but Anakin is coming perilously close. When he is assigned to protect the woman he has loved since childhood, he is torn between love and duty. The Jedi discipline does not seem to help him as it does the others, so his loyalties are put to the test: Will he insist on being an exception to the rules of the Jedi Order?

On Coruscant, Anakin suspects that Padmé has feelings for him. On Naboo, where Anakin's charm is in full force, Padme's feelings become transparent—but the inherent danger of their passions frightens both Senator and Jedi.

When Anakin senses his mother in terrible pain, Padmé goes with him to Tatooine in search of her. After Anakin fails to rescue Shmi in time, Padmé must alleviate the Padawan's anger, resentment, and despair.

In Anakin's mind, it is his own lack of resolve and strength that has failed his mother and cost him so much pain. At his mother's grave, marked by a black stone, Anakin makes a silent vow to build his strength until nothing can withstand his power.

Electromotive power lines

Interface module links wiring to nerves

Sensory impulse lines

Fingertips electrostatically sensitive to touch

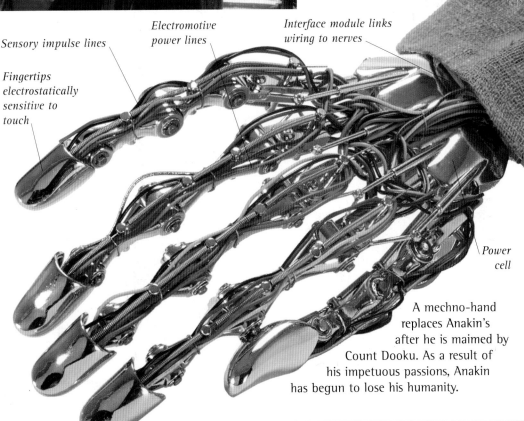

Power cell

DATA FILE

◆ Anakin has started the study of lightsaber Form IV, known for its power.

◆ The pain of life-draining Sith lightning is an experience of evil that Anakin will never forget.

A mechno-hand replaces Anakin's after he is maimed by Count Dooku. As a result of his impetuous passions, Anakin has begun to lose his humanity.

Zam Wesell

As a CLAWDITE SHAPE-SHIFTER, Zam Wesell can change her appearance to mimic a range of humanoid forms, giving her a special edge as a hired assassin. Zam learned her trade on Denon, the globe-girdling metropolis second only to Coruscant as a center of galactic business. In the high-risk world of industrial espionage, Zam rose from corporate security sergeant to executive bodyguard before seeking higher fees for contract execution and bounty hunting.

ASN-121
ASSASSIN DROID

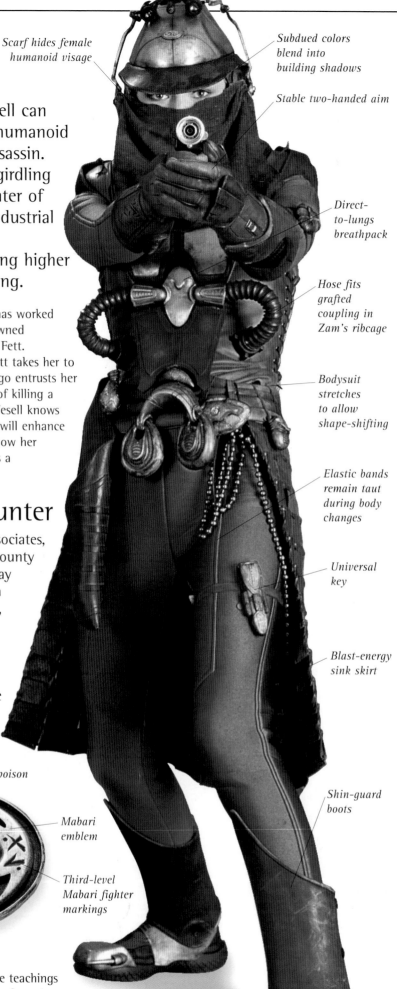

Scarf hides female humanoid visage

Subdued colors blend into building shadows

Stable two-handed aim

Direct-to-lungs breathpack

Hose fits grafted coupling in Zam's ribcage

Bodysuit stretches to allow shape-shifting

Elastic bands remain taut during body changes

Universal key

Blast-energy sink skirt

Shin-guard boots

Boots accept a variety of limb forms

For some years Zam has worked on and off with renowned bounty hunter Jango Fett. Her latest job with Fett takes her to Coruscant, where Jango entrusts her with the assignment of killing a prominent Senator. Wesell knows that this opportunity will enhance her reputation and allow her to return to Denon as a master in her field.

Bounty Hunter

A loner with few close associates, Zam Wesell is typical of bounty hunters. She inhabits a gray zone that extends to both sides of the law. Arrogant, highly skilled, and feeling unchallenged by legal bodyguard and security work, Wesell regards bounty hunting as a more suitable channel for her superior talent.

Stinger painful but not fatal

Bite delivers lethal nerve poison

KOUHUNS
Zam uses two deadly kouhuns for her Senatorial assassination job. Small, silent arthropods like the kouhuns of Indoumodo can evade even tight security. Unlike projectiles or energy weapons, they are virtually impossible to trace back to their users. Kouhuns are starved in advance, so they head straight for warm-blooded life forms when released, and use a fast-acting nerve toxin to kill their prey.

Mabari emblem

Third-level Mabari fighter markings

CAPE SEAL

Zam's discipline derives from the teachings of the Mabari, an ancient order of warrior-knights on her homeworld. She wears Mabari inscriptions and stylized emblems, including a cape seal that is an ancient Mabari artifact.

To prevent being traced, Zam Wesell prefers to steal a new vehicle for each new job. But when her security depends on performance she uses her own airspeeder.

Streamlined with enclosed cockpit for high speeds

Cleaning rod

Electromagnetic pulse barrel

Secret compartment for sniper rifle

Waste heat and radiation radiator

Zam favors her KYD-21 blaster pistol for both attack and defense, though Jango has begun teaching her that projectile weapons can be useful when working invisibly in the dark.

Igniter pin

Hadrium alloy

Muzzle brake absorbs emitter flash

Embedding prongs

Injector needle

Blaster gas capsule loading port

Guardless trigger for fast action

Poison chamber

Stabilizing fins

Handle holds power cell

KYD-21 Blaster

Though she carries a projectile rifle at Jango's insistence, Zam's primary weapon is a compact, precise KYD-21 pistol. She finds she can hide a pistol more easily when she needs to disguise herself as a non-threatening presence in order to close in on her mark.

Under intense Jedi mind-pressure, Zam begins to reveal her employer...until she is silenced by an assassin.

SABERDART
Preferring to leave no trace, Zam dislikes projectile weapons. A saberdart such as Jango might use may be silent and highly lethal, but has the potential to lead pursuers back to its source.

Visor cuts glare

Light helmet

Comlink system

Scrambled direct comlink pickup to Jango Fett

Clawdite shape-shifters, or "changelings," evolved on a world inhabited by warring humanoid subspecies. Shape-shifters developed the ability to mimic the appearance of other species in order to blend in without being killed. As a changeling dies, its ability to shape-shift fades and it returns to a neutral Clawdite configuration.

Flexible armorweave jerkin

PROJECTILE RIFLE

Simple optical scope

High Stakes

Zam knows that in accepting a risky assignment from Jango Fett, she is in danger of being used as an expendable pawn. Such are the risks of the high-stakes trade in death, and Zam is prepared to take them...though she will find that she is not equipped to outrun two Jedi.

Power amplifier circuitry

DATA FILE

◆ Shape-shifting takes effort, and it is only through long practice that Zam has learned to rest in a mimicked form.

◆ Although shape-shifters are most effective at a limited range of shapes they imitate often, medical assistance can enhance their abilities much further.

Recoil-damping stock

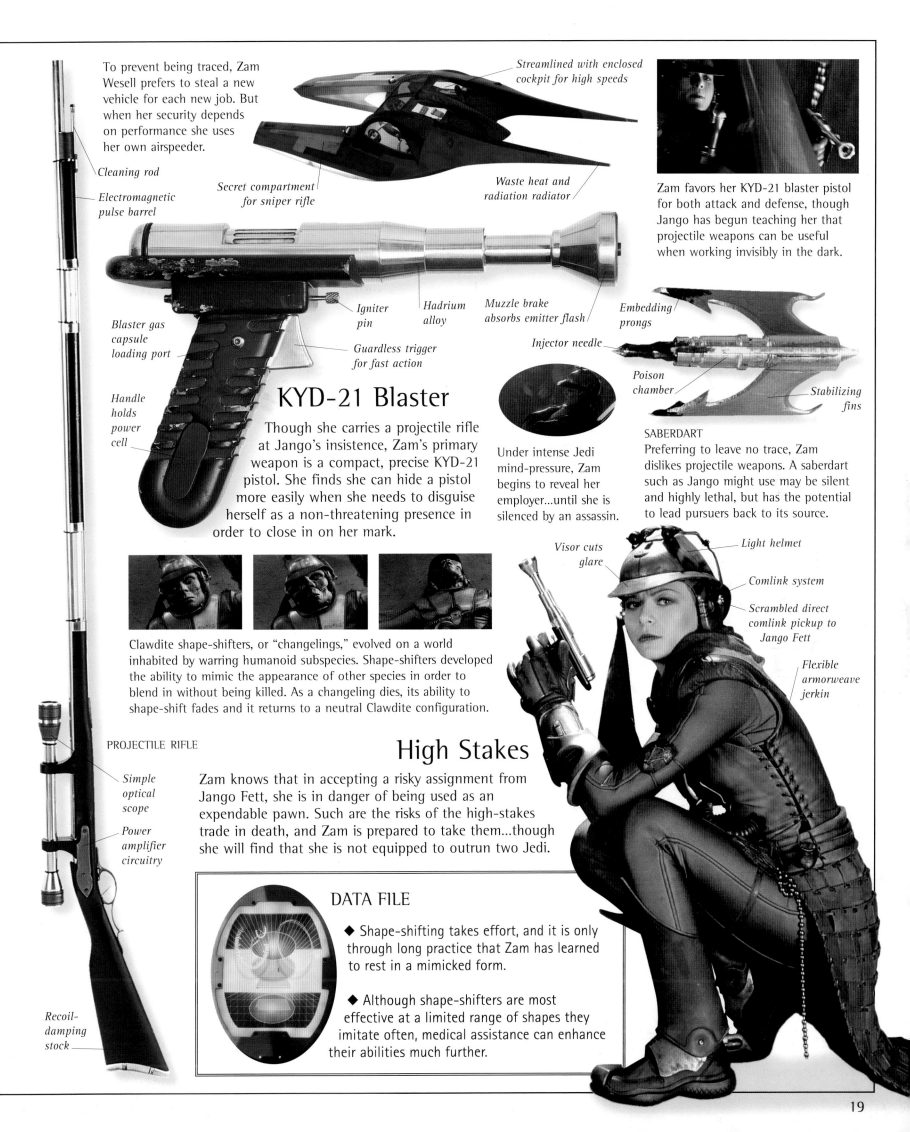

Coruscant Underlevels

POCKET BLASTER
Laser sight

Eye threads

Vigilante wardman

Head knots

Handmade combat vest

LYING HUNDREDS OF STORIES below the skyscraper pinnacles, Coruscant's urban canyon floors never see the light of day. A realm of artificial illumination, the lower levels of the galaxy's largest city are the only affordable areas for many of the planet's citizens. Rumbling with machines that serve the elite above, its streets haunted by exploiters and thugs, and its walls riddled with weird vermin, Coruscant's underworld toughens the strong and consumes the weak.

Klatooinian hired enforcer

Duracrete worm hide

In spite of their appearance, many of the buildings in Coruscant's underlevels are centuries old. Droid crews maintain some sections beautifully, but other parts are left to decay.

Impoverished Bith

Sporran shielding

Discarded clothing

Beyond Law

Coruscant's underlevels harbor a larger population than do many entire star sectors, leaving millions beyond the effective protection of Coruscant's security force. Local neighborhoods may fall to the mercy of hired thugs and extortionists. But the toughest faces sometimes belong to vigilantes, who choose to defend the people on their own turf from criminals who would abuse them.

Underlevel Coruscanti hail from all parts of the galaxy. Many immigrants arrive with only a small case of belongings from their homeworlds, little prepared for the challenges they find.

Cheap, general humanoid boots

Shinplates

DATA FILE

◆ Off-world disposal of garbage is expensive, so much refuse is compressed into blocks and transported down to fill the deepest parts of the underlevels.

◆ The only effective extermination method for an infestation of stone-mite trionts makes use of an oxidizer foam to rust them to death.

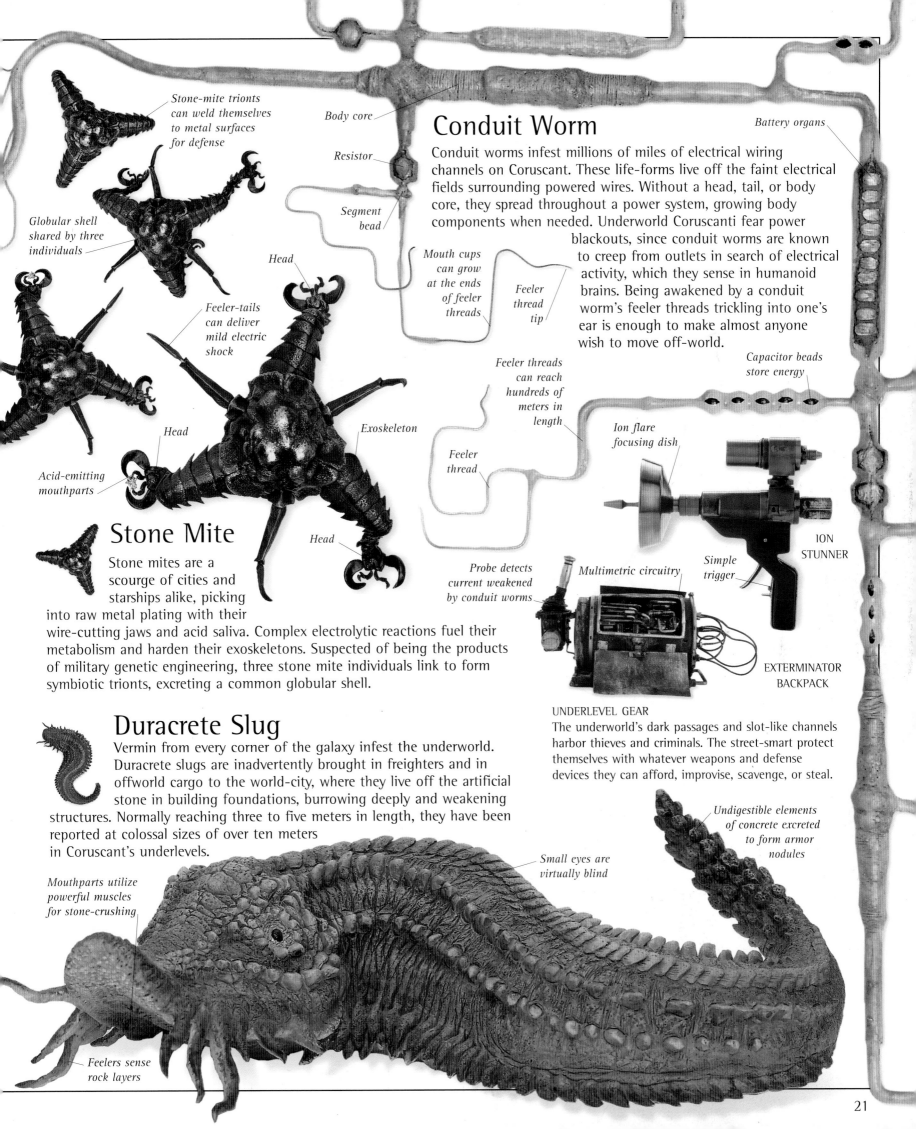

Stone-mite trions can weld themselves to metal surfaces for defense

Body core

Resistor

Segment bead

Conduit Worm

Conduit worms infest millions of miles of electrical wiring channels on Coruscant. These life-forms live off the faint electrical fields surrounding powered wires. Without a head, tail, or body core, they spread throughout a power system, growing body components when needed. Underworld Coruscanti fear power blackouts, since conduit worms are known to creep from outlets in search of electrical activity, which they sense in humanoid brains. Being awakened by a conduit worm's feeler threads trickling into one's ear is enough to make almost anyone wish to move off-world.

Battery organs

Globular shell shared by three individuals

Head

Feeler-tails can deliver mild electric shock

Mouth cups can grow at the ends of feeler threads

Feeler thread tip

Capacitor beads store energy

Feeler threads can reach hundreds of meters in length

Ion flare focusing dish

Head

Exoskeleton

Feeler thread

Acid-emitting mouthparts

Head

Stone Mite

Stone mites are a scourge of cities and starships alike, picking into raw metal plating with their wire-cutting jaws and acid saliva. Complex electrolytic reactions fuel their metabolism and harden their exoskeletons. Suspected of being the products of military genetic engineering, three stone mite individuals link to form symbiotic trions, excreting a common globular shell.

Probe detects current weakened by conduit worms

Multimetric circuitry

Simple trigger

ION STUNNER

EXTERMINATOR BACKPACK

Duracrete Slug

Vermin from every corner of the galaxy infest the underworld. Duracrete slugs are inadvertently brought in freighters and in offworld cargo to the world-city, where they live off the artificial stone in building foundations, burrowing deeply and weakening structures. Normally reaching three to five meters in length, they have been reported at colossal sizes of over ten meters in Coruscant's underlevels.

UNDERLEVEL GEAR

The underworld's dark passages and slot-like channels harbor thieves and criminals. The street-smart protect themselves with whatever weapons and defense devices they can afford, improvise, scavenge, or steal.

Undigestible elements of concrete excreted to form armor nodules

Small eyes are virtually blind

Mouthparts utilize powerful muscles for stone-crushing

Feelers sense rock layers

Outlander Nightclub

AGAINST THE SPECTACULAR BACKDROP of the largest city in the galaxy, the Outlander provides a setting for a wide variety of purposes. While some patrons pass through its doors just to have a good time, most are in search of something else: a companion, a sale, or someone to con. Weaving among the would-be glitterati are low-lifes and criminals searching for gullible victims to exploit. For all of them, the gambling club is a place that makes the rest of the world fade away. To an assassin on the run, the Outlander is a potential haven—if Zam can somehow lose the pursuing Jedi among the crowd.

Human hair wig

Thoadeye-style makeup

Obi-Wan and Anakin exercise subtle teamwork when they trail Zam to the Outlander. Anakin enters the crowd to flush out the target while Obi-Wan bides his time, waiting for Wesell to make her move.

"Starshine special" additive given only for the right wink

Color-coded basic drink components

Central liquid-processing unit

Aludium pu-36

Polyquaternium-7 multicarbonator

Insecticide

The Right Mix

What one species might find a good drink may be a lethal poison to the next creature who steps up to the bar. To avoid a lawsuit on the lawyer-ridden planet of Coruscant, most small nightclubs play safe by serving minimum-risk, watered-down drinks. Trusted regulars receive much better service and far more interesting concoctions.

Patrons

The Outlander attracts a mostly humanoid clientele. Pan-species clubs are only for the truly determined and stout of heart, as humans tend to feel uncomfortable at clubs designed for quasi-ambulatory plant wads accustomed to living in shallow water—and vice-versa.

Height-enhancing shoes of hired dancer

Solloops
hairstyle

Flexible antenepalps
concealed under hair

The pursuit of fashion can be desperately confusing amid the vast populations of Coruscant, and even a Jedi's ancient traditional tunic does not stand out in the Outlander crowd.

Petrified hairstyle

Surgically
altered eye color

Cult tattoo
betrays affiliation

Gesture of influence

Slythmongers

Low-lifes who peddle cheap narcotics manufactured by disbarred pharmacists are called slythmongers on Coruscant. A few are likely to show up at any average club. Slythmongers must be prepared for a quick exit when customers have a bad or fatal reaction to the latest, most fashionable concoction.

Cilona-extract "death sticks" are powerful narcotics. Each successive dose literally shortens the user's lifespan in increasingly large intervals.

Two grades of cilona
for adding to drinks

DEATH STICKS

Faytonni

Accent gas
emitter

Masked
Weequay

Chiller
surface

Hidden
knockout
drops

Long
overcoat
conceals
illegal
chemicals
for sale

Heat
exchange
vanes

Soluble
zoosha
fabric

Con artists merge into the crowd at the nightclub. Tonight's miscreants include a professional kidnapper, a crime lord's enforcer, and the unconvincing "Lieutenant" Faytonni dressed in a stolen military uniform.

Refrigeration
tubes

DRINKS CHILLER

Shoes contain
secret storage
for contraband

DATA FILE

◆ When club owners spike drink-synthesizer tanks with liquids such as medical sterilizers or hydraulic fluid, the "unique" resulting concoctions can bring a flood of new customers—or a deluge of lawsuits.

Dexter's Diner

AFTER BOUNTY HUNTER Zam Wesell is killed by a mysterious toxic saberdart, Obi-Wan Kenobi heads for the haunt of a four-armed Besalisk named Dexter Jettster. Dexter's unassuming diner serves more than hearty food—favored diners can also obtain nuggets of precious information. The brusque but good-hearted Jettster has a checkered past with expeditionary oil-harvesting crews across the galaxy. He spent many years manning rigs, tending bar, cooking chow, brawling, dealing in contraband, and running weapons on the side to disaffected locals. On Coruscant, Dexter has made a fresh start with his diner and enjoys his stable and straightforward new employment.

Within the endless metropolis of Coruscant, the "world of worlds," one can find nearly anything if one knows where to look. Well off the fashionable dining routes, in a business and manufacturing district, lies the small installation known as Dexter's Diner.

The spirited antique Droid Waitress, WA-7, serves Dexter and his clientele with officious precision.

Four large arms require hearty metabolism

Decorative skirt

Built-in order transmitter

Hermione's belt

Voice reader

Upper-hands are dominant manipulators

Retaining cord

Record stylus

Repulsor stabilizer

ORDER COMM

Diner logo

Agile unipod wheel

Lower-hands are secondary graspers

Lucky washrag

Dexter's cooking provides an alternative to Coruscant's often bizarre menus. It was the unidentifiable "vercupti of sgazza boleruueé" on the Jedi Temple Main House menu one day that drove Obi-Wan to try the diner, and rekindle his friendship with Dexter Jettster.

Dress style harks back to earlier time

Hermione Bagwa

Dexter's waitress, Hermione Bagwa, duels with WA-7 for mastery of the dining room. Each is convinced that she has the superior position. Hermione grew up in the Coruscant underlevels and feels very fortunate to work on the surface now.

Boots offer protection from toxic kitchen slops

DATA FILE

◆ Regulars at Dexter's Diner debate the degree to which the menu's distinctive "special recipes" are influenced by Dexter's background in mining sluices and industrial lubricants.

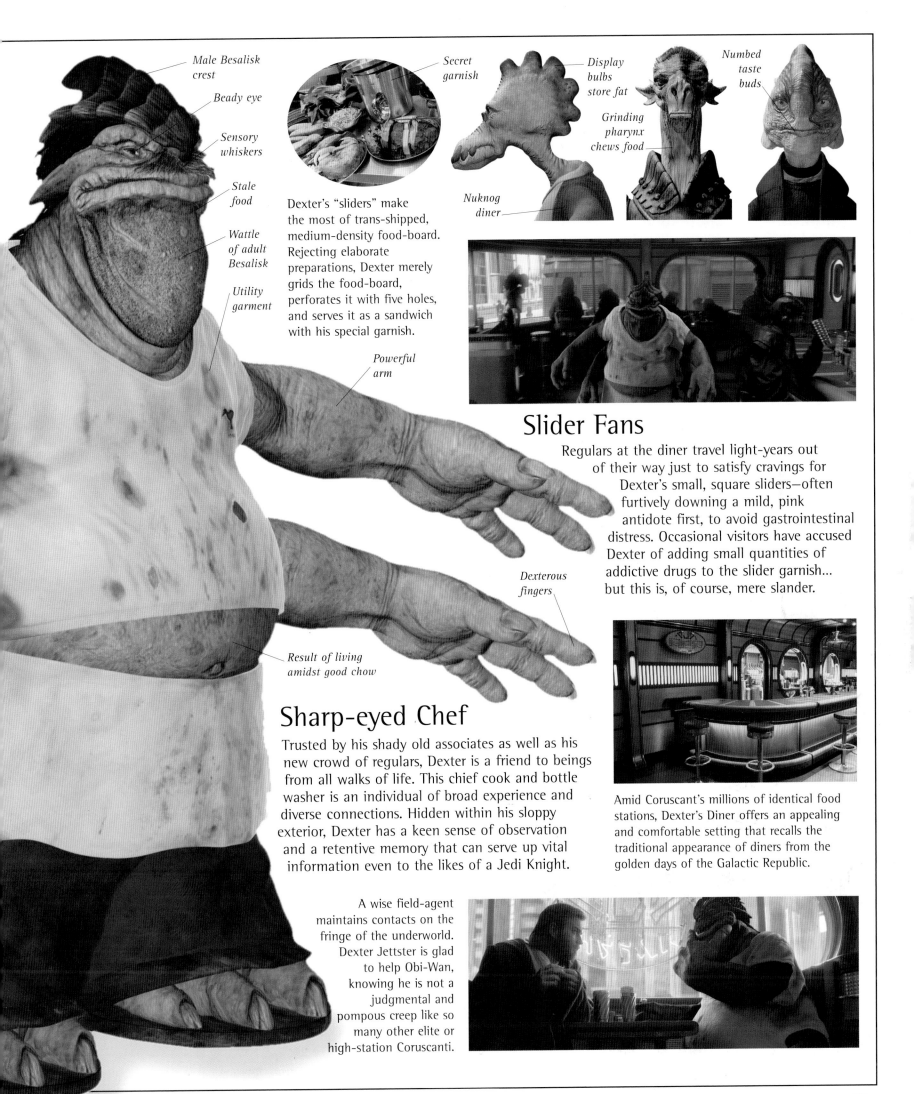

Male Besalisk
crest

Beady eye

Sensory
whiskers

Stale
food

Wattle
of adult
Besalisk

Utility
garment

Secret
garnish

Dexter's "sliders" make
the most of trans-shipped,
medium-density food-board.
Rejecting elaborate
preparations, Dexter merely
grids the food-board,
perforates it with five holes,
and serves it as a sandwich
with his special garnish.

Display
bulbs
store fat

Grinding
pharynx
chews food

Numbed
taste
buds

Nuknog
diner

Powerful
arm

Dexterous
fingers

Result of living
amidst good chow

Slider Fans

Regulars at the diner travel light-years out
of their way just to satisfy cravings for
Dexter's small, square sliders—often
furtively downing a mild, pink
antidote first, to avoid gastrointestinal
distress. Occasional visitors have accused
Dexter of adding small quantities of
addictive drugs to the slider garnish...
but this is, of course, mere slander.

Sharp-eyed Chef

Trusted by his shady old associates as well as his
new crowd of regulars, Dexter is a friend to beings
from all walks of life. This chief cook and bottle
washer is an individual of broad experience and
diverse connections. Hidden within his sloppy
exterior, Dexter has a keen sense of observation
and a retentive memory that can serve up vital
information even to the likes of a Jedi Knight.

Amid Coruscant's millions of identical food
stations, Dexter's Diner offers an appealing
and comfortable setting that recalls the
traditional appearance of diners from the
golden days of the Galactic Republic.

A wise field-agent
maintains contacts on the
fringe of the underworld.
Dexter Jettster is glad
to help Obi-Wan,
knowing he is not a
judgmental and
pompous creep like so
many other elite or
high-station Coruscanti.

Jedi Temple

FOR MILLENNIA the Jedi Temple on Coruscant has served as the training ground and home base of the Jedi Knights, peacekeeping defenders of justice throughout the galaxy. At the Temple, Jedi initiates learn the ways of the Force, a mystical energy field created by all living things. Hundreds of other individuals who are not Jedi Knights provide vital support in everything from operations management to technical analysis. The galaxy is so large that complete law enforcement is impossible; so most Jedi rove through assigned regions on "journey missions," empowered to support justice as they see fit. Jedi based at the Temple travel on special assignments.

The Jedi Temple on Coruscant occupies hallowed ground sanctified by the noble efforts of Jedi dating back many thousands of years into remote antiquity.

Jedi Padawan with learner braid

Traditional Jedi robes

Natural skin coloration

The Jedi eschew materialism as they do any attachments that could cloud their judgment. Yoda's years of dedication have raised him to power and influence, but he meets his colleagues in a simple cell.

Visually disruptive patterning

Active Jedi

Jedi begin their lifelong training when they are recognized as gifted children. They accept a life of total dedication and self-sacrifice to become diplomat-warriors. As initiates, they train together until they are accepted as Padawans, or apprentice learners. They must then face the Trials to become Jedi Knights, who are allowed in turn to take on an apprentice and earn the title of Master.

Gesture of patience

Diplomatic boots less rugged than field-agent boots

Shaak Ti

Jedi come from every corner of the galaxy. Jedi Master Shaak Ti is a Togruta, a species which lives in dense tribes on the planet Shili, where the disruptive coloration of their long lekku (head-tails) serves to confuse predators. Unlike most of her kind, Shaak Ti is a highly independent spirit.

Yoda

THE WISE YODA is the sole member of the Jedi Council to recognize the present danger of Jedi complacency. Yoda sees that, in these troubled times, the greatest challenge may come from within the system itself. Even at his advanced age and with his formidable reputation and responsibilities, Yoda still trains young initiates. His students are taught to take nothing for granted and to keep their minds open to every possibility, avoiding the pitfalls of overconfidence.

Obi-Wan Kenobi has grown close to Yoda since the death of Kenobi's Jedi Master, Qui-Gon Jinn. Facing a difficulty in his current assignment, Obi-Wan does not hesitate to consult with his wise friend and colleague, who in turn uses the opportunity as an exercise for his young Jedi initiates.

Short Padawan haircut

Bear Clan member

Low-power "safety blade" generator

TRAINING LIGHTSABER

Sensitive ears complement Yoda's habit of listening more than talking

Hand gestures help focus mental use of the Force

Adjustable-opacity faceplate

NOVICE HELMET
Young initiates wear helmets that mask their vision, training them to see using the Force rather than their bodily senses alone.

JEDI INITIATES

Hidden Strengths

Yoda's capabilities with the Force give him amazing strength and speed, as well as the ability to levitate. These special powers, combined with his knowledge of fighting tactics, allow him to overcome virtually any opponent, though times are few indeed that Yoda has actually used his lightsaber in combat.

Simple robe is a sincere expression of humility, despite Yoda's great power and reputation

DATA FILE

◆ More than 9,000 fully trained Jedi are scattered throughout the galaxy, with a further 200 available at the Jedi Temple for emergency missions.

◆ Yoda has never revealed his homeworld, and his species is rarely seen anywhere in the galaxy.

Jedi Archives

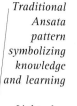

EVER SINCE the ancient origins of the Jedi Order, knowledge and its mastery have been vital to the Jedi mission of supporting peace and justice throughout the Republic. The great Archives Library in the Jedi Temple safeguards the accumulated knowledge gathered by millions of individuals over hundreds of generations. It is a repository of seemingly infinite information on every part of the known galaxy and on billions upon billions of its inhabitants. The Archives is the greatest library in the Republic, and an incomparable asset to the Jedi, whether they are acting as diplomats, counselors, or fighters.

The Main Hall of the Jedi Archives holds most of its information in holobooks to prevent electronic access by overly curious outsiders. Some of the holobooks date back many thousands of years to the earliest days of the Galactic Republic.

Chon Actrion, "Architect of Freedom"

The Archives offers many opportunities for reflection. Statues remind Jedi not only of the great and the good, but also of the "Lost 20"—the only Jedi to leave the Order voluntarily.

Simple plinth

Jocasta Nu

Madame Jocasta Nu is Archives Director and a former active Jedi Knight. Her astonishing memory seems to rival the Archives itself, which she runs as a tool rather than a service, expecting Jedi and support personnel to do their own research. Her pride sometimes blinds her to the Archives' limitations, however.

Full robe worn by Nu in elder years

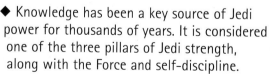

DATA FILE

◆ Knowledge has been a key source of Jedi power for thousands of years. It is considered one of the three pillars of Jedi strength, along with the Force and self-discipline.

◆ Holobooks are an ancient self-contained technology requiring only small amounts of energy. They are easy to use and offer many modes of interaction with their users.

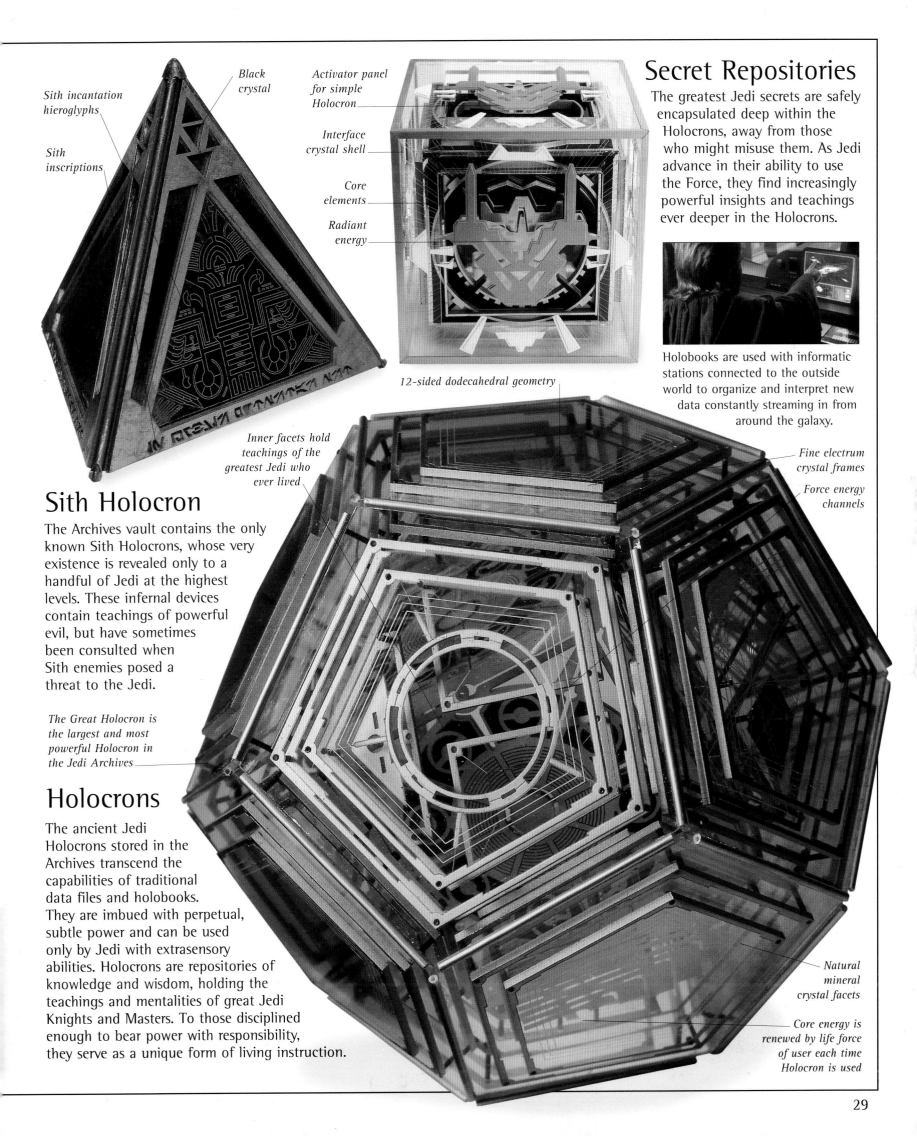

Sith incantation hieroglyphs

Sith inscriptions

Black crystal

Activator panel for simple Holocron

Interface crystal shell

Core elements

Radiant energy

Secret Repositories

The greatest Jedi secrets are safely encapsulated deep within the Holocrons, away from those who might misuse them. As Jedi advance in their ability to use the Force, they find increasingly powerful insights and teachings ever deeper in the Holocrons.

Holobooks are used with informatic stations connected to the outside world to organize and interpret new data constantly streaming in from around the galaxy.

12-sided dodecahedral geometry

Inner facets hold teachings of the greatest Jedi who ever lived

Fine electrum crystal frames

Force energy channels

Sith Holocron

The Archives vault contains the only known Sith Holocrons, whose very existence is revealed only to a handful of Jedi at the highest levels. These infernal devices contain teachings of powerful evil, but have sometimes been consulted when Sith enemies posed a threat to the Jedi.

The Great Holocron is the largest and most powerful Holocron in the Jedi Archives

Holocrons

The ancient Jedi Holocrons stored in the Archives transcend the capabilities of traditional data files and holobooks. They are imbued with perpetual, subtle power and can be used only by Jedi with extrasensory abilities. Holocrons are repositories of knowledge and wisdom, holding the teachings and mentalities of great Jedi Knights and Masters. To those disciplined enough to bear power with responsibility, they serve as a unique form of living instruction.

Natural mineral crystal facets

Core energy is renewed by life force of user each time Holocron is used

Freighter Trampers

FOR CENTURIES Coruscant has attracted immigrants in search of seemingly infinite opportunities. As the present turmoil leaves individuals uncertain of their future, many are now heading back to their homeworlds or further out into the galaxy in search of new employment. Among these migrants are the freighter trampers, so-called because they commute from job to job on the freighter lanes. The trampers form a community of their own, and such a diverse mix forms an ideal environment in which Anakin and Padmé may travel unnoticed.

Cramped quarters

On the freighter, Padmé travels with a minimum of belongings, as she is no longer required to wear the formal attire of political office.

Concealed stun baton

Steerage overseers have the authority to strand miscreants on any passing star system. These harsh measures serve to keep the freighter trampers in line.

Space freighter at docking bay | *Crowded platform*

Coruscant Spaceport

On Coruscant, space freighters with heavy drive engines are allowed to land only at spaceports. Coruscant's stiff engine-maintenance regulations and powerful damper fields make its docking bays less radioative than those on less-developed planets. Always heavily traveled, the Coruscant spaceports are beginning to strain toward capacity as more passengers sign on for transit off-world.

Filter for polluted air in steerage

Donovian rainmen wear distinctive rain hoods. The rainmen service signal towers over the rugged terrain of Donovia, a planet mined for many precious materials.

Backpack transponder for mining scout

Housing made of bedpan

Welder made from diatomic bomb igniter

TRAMPER GEAR
Freighter trampers barter with each other for the goods in their possession, and often recombine components of disparate origins into workable equipment, or "tramper gear."

Hood allows close work in rain

Tired electrician awaiting next job

Journeyman-team foreman signaling availability for work

Sealer's kit

Traveling in disguise aboard the freighter *Jendirian Valley*, Anakin and Padmé mix with ordinary people, unhindered by their usual professional personae.

C00-series cookdroid

Freighter food is the epitome of utility nourishment. Cookdroids are programmed to use the most basic and inexpensive recipes, which ensures that a wide variety of humanoids and aliens will find the food edible.

Economic Refugees

Many freighter trampers indenture themselves to corporations in order to earn the cost of their passage to new worlds in search of work. However, many find that when they arrive, the long-hoped-for employment has disappeared. They then have to indenture themselves for a second passage to another world, starting a cycle in which millions live in a form of bondage little different from slavery.

Raddan vermin-killer's vest

Spellsayer's teardrop emblem

Pants cover protective undergarments

TRAMPER DRESS
Freighter trampers sport a bewildering array of clothing, indicating various specialized professions, callings, or cultures.

Reactor tender's gear

Breath mask filters out radioactive gases

Coverings expose as little flesh as possible

Lead-impregnated clothing acts as shielding

Mutant Aqualish with second pair of eyes

Nuclear-waste technician's garb

DATA FILE

◆ Seasoned freighter trampers can quickly spot a batch of fresh synthetic vegetables on a tray of preservative-loaded food that may be years old.

◆ Freighter passengers are now leaving Coruscant at a rate that would depopulate an ordinary planet in one standard month.

Padmé Naberrie

WHEN PADMÉ NABERRIE last saw Anakin Skywalker, he was just a boy, though she sensed something special about him even then. Now that Anakin has re-entered her life, Padmé is amazed at the effect the young Jedi has on her. She senses a connection that overcomes all her efforts to deny it, a feeling in conflict with her dedication and determination to serve her people. Her increasingly dangerous life and her exposure to the death of loved ones force Padmé to realise how precious every minute is. At the crucial moment, she becomes determined to live as fully as possible no matter what the consequences—and if she is to be destroyed, she will go down fighting.

Formal court hairstyle

Processor status indicators

Camera eye

Spotlight and holoprojector

After her years in political service, the planetary government complex on Naboo serves as a familiar walking place for Padmé.

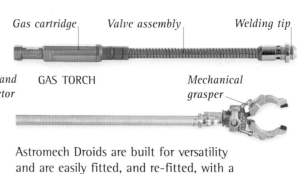

Padmé's family home in the Lake Country is called Varykino. It is here that she feels safest and can most be herself.

Gas cartridge　　*Valve assembly*　　*Welding tip*

GAS TORCH

Mechanical grasper

Astromech Droids are built for versatility and are easily fitted, and re-fitted, with a range of standardized parts and equipment.

Rocket assembly

Symbol

All high offices on Naboo are elective, yet they carry with them the complex dress codes associated with hereditary nobility. Padmé accepts the symbolic value of such trappings but would prefer to wear clothes that express her own identity.

Actuator　　*Capacitor*　　*Extensor rod*

Polydigital grasper

R2-D2

Padmé is faithfully attended by R2-D2, an Astromech Droid that regularly exceed its programming in loyal service. While droids are disregarded through most of the galaxy, on open-hearted Naboo, Padmé is not unusual in feeling an affection for a mechanical servant who seems so spirited.

Retractable third leg

Sensory impulse cable

When Padmé returns from Coruscant, she consults with Queen Jamillia in Theed's Royal Palace. There, her old colleagues and political advisors struggle with small Naboo's surprisingly important role in the wider world of galactic politics.

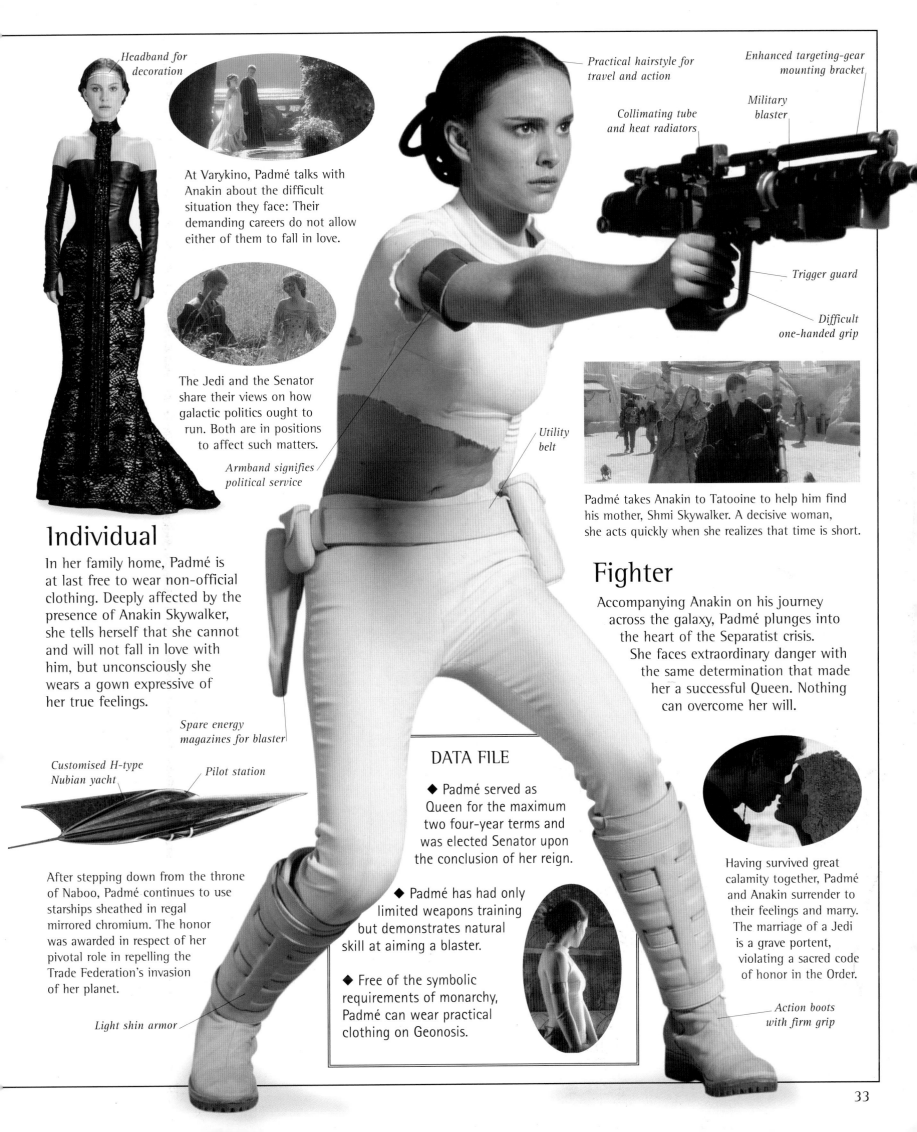

Headband for
decoration

At Varykino, Padmé talks with
Anakin about the difficult
situation they face: Their
demanding careers do not allow
either of them to fall in love.

The Jedi and the Senator
share their views on how
galactic politics ought to
run. Both are in positions
to affect such matters.

Armband signifies
political service

Practical hairstyle for
travel and action

Collimating tube
and heat radiators

Enhanced targeting-gear
mounting bracket

Military
blaster

Trigger guard

Difficult
one-handed grip

Utility
belt

Padmé takes Anakin to Tatooine to help him find
his mother, Shmi Skywalker. A decisive woman,
she acts quickly when she realizes that time is short.

Individual

In her family home, Padmé is
at last free to wear non-official
clothing. Deeply affected by the
presence of Anakin Skywalker,
she tells herself that she cannot
and will not fall in love with
him, but unconsciously she
wears a gown expressive of
her true feelings.

Spare energy
magazines for blaster

Customised H-type
Nubian yacht

Pilot station

After stepping down from the throne
of Naboo, Padmé continues to use
starships sheathed in regal
mirrored chromium. The honor
was awarded in respect of her
pivotal role in repelling the
Trade Federation's invasion
of her planet.

Light shin armor

Fighter

Accompanying Anakin on his journey
across the galaxy, Padmé plunges into
the heart of the Separatist crisis.
She faces extraordinary danger with
the same determination that made
her a successful Queen. Nothing
can overcome her will.

DATA FILE

◆ Padmé served as
Queen for the maximum
two four-year terms and
was elected Senator upon
the conclusion of her reign.

◆ Padmé has had only
limited weapons training
but demonstrates natural
skill at aiming a blaster.

◆ Free of the symbolic
requirements of monarchy,
Padmé can wear practical
clothing on Geonosis.

Having survived great
calamity together, Padmé
and Anakin surrender to
their feelings and marry.
The marriage of a Jedi
is a grave portent,
violating a sacred code
of honor in the Order.

Action boots
with firm grip

Kaminoans

WHEN A GLOBAL CLIMATE SHIFT flooded their planet, the Kaminoans were forced to adapt. They developed cloning technology and practised selective breeding to keep their race alive. As a result of the hardships endured during the Great Flood, the Kaminoans have an austere, non-materialist outlook. They are outwardly polite, yet behind this lurks an extreme intolerance of physical imperfection. The Kaminoans are reliant on certain outworld technologies and raw materials to maintain their advanced society, so they use their cloning abilities to produce goods for export. When a Jedi named Sifo-Dyas placed an order for a massive clone army a decade ago, the Kaminoans embarked upon the largest human cloning project ever undertaken.

Large eyes see well in murky conditions

KO SAI

Elongated bones allow limited flexibility in neck

TAUN WE

Long neck consists of seven elongated bones

Female Kaminoans lack headcrest

The planet Kamino once had extensive land areas, but the melting of inland continental glaciers sank all land beneath the waves. Today, only the Kaminoan stilt cities project above the water, forming colonies of varying sizes around the planet.

Black body-glove underlayer

Clone serum test probe

Clone science emblem

Serum sample pouch

Black cuff is a mark of honor; scientific rank indicated by thickness

Spongy wings

Kaminoan saddle rig

Skull contains buoyancy chambers

Sieve plates filter plankton underwater or in flight

Kaminoans use domesticated aiwhas for sport and transportation between close-sited colonies. These animals can fly and swim with equal ease, controlling their density using a water-vascular system. This system allows the aiwhas to fill their spongy tissues with seawater when they want to swim underwater, and to wring the water out and shed it to lighten themselves for flight.

Obi-Wan Kenobi identifies himself as a Jedi to Kamino Space Traffic Control on his way in and, upon landing, is met by the Prime Minister's assistant.

Project Leaders

Ministerial assistant Taun We serves as a Project Coordinator for the clone army. Taun We has studied human emotional psychology to ensure that the clones are developed into mentally stable individuals. Chief Scientist Ko Sai, serene yet exacting, oversees the clone-army project's biological aspects, ensuring that clones are of the highest quality. She also supervizes the delicate redesign of the genetic codes that make the clones independently intelligent, but preconditioned for obedience. No other scientist in the galaxy could so capably manipulate the genes of another species.

Dexterous fingers

Kamino's prime minister, Lama Su, is well aware of the clone army's importance to his economy. He personally meets the Jedi whom he thinks has come to inspect it.

Lama Su is unsure whether Obi-Wan Kenobi's seeming ignorance of the tremendous clone army is a devious test or a complex form of politeness. Regardless, his overriding concern in meeting with Kenobi is to ensure that the Kaminoans will obtain their first shipment bonus payment, so he makes nothing of the Jedi's odd behaviour.

Kaminoan stilt cities echo the Kaminoans' former land colonies. These were communal dwellings constructed of wattle and daub, which shed water easily in the long storm seasons.

White form-fitting clothing

Cloak of office

Digitigrade configuration of feet adds height

Small feet adapted to firm Kaminoan seabeds and now to hard flooring

TIPOCA (KAMINOAN CAPITAL CITY)

Communications tower

Static discharge towers vital during electrical storms

Streamlined outer shell sheds water and wind

Pylons present minimal silhouette to avoid wave battering

Pylons embedded in shallow continental shelf below

Clone Trooper Growth

CLONE ARMY PROJECT EMBLEM

THE MYSTERIOUS Jedi Sifo-Dyas ordered from the Kaminoan cloners a secret army created from a single individual. An agent named Tyranus selected the clone-source: Jango Fett, a man whose natural combat ability and high endurance level would produce the ideal soldier. Under Kaminoan Chief Scientist Ko Sai, the clones' genetic code was altered to accelerate their growth to twice the normal human rate, and their mental structure was subtly reconfigured to make them obedient to authority. Comprehensive training shapes the identity and abilities of the clones throughout their development. The result of this colossal project is an army of identical soldiers produced in a world of clinical efficiency.

Most Kaminoans regard the clones as laboratory specimens but Taun We feels some affection for the young cadets.

The clones begin life as artificially created embryos that are mass-produced in the Egg Lab.

Odd-class helmet has gold plating

Broadcast signal receiver

Broadcast power receiver

Durable inert plastoid helmet

Anodized-color equipment for even-class helmet

EVEN-CLASS HELMET

Mental receptivity enhancer

ODD-CLASS HELMET
The clones wear special learning helmets, which are color coded to reflect odd or even numbering. Odd or even is the only identity distinction the clones are allowed.

Biorhythm synchronizer

Earphone silences external sounds to provide isolated audio environment for learning

Accelerated Learning

Clone youths grow at twice the rate of ordinary humans, so they crave information but receive only half the normal time to assimilate it. This loss of life-experience is compensated for by a learning program that focuses more on military knowledge than on academics. In addition, special equipment modulates brainwaves and enhances the clones' ability to retain instruction.

Pickup reads vocal responses

Maintaining Perfection

The Kaminoans strive to control every aspect of the clones' existence for perfect regularity, but slight deviations occur in the development of any living individual's biochemistry. Chief Scientist Ko Sai inspects the clones at every stage of life to identify those who have drifted from the standard. Aberrant clones are given extra conditioning to regularize them.

Brainwave probe

Brainwave canceler

SERUM GUN

Analysis chamber

Sampling graspers

Clone birth pod

Reorientation unit

Cord used for symbolic honor training

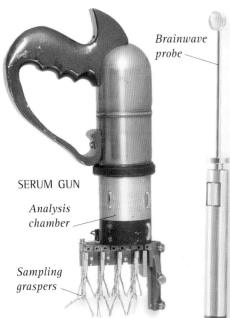

Blank character and accelerated growth shape clone face slightly differently from clone-source

Utility garments in security bicolor style

The Kaminoans' dedication to perfection has led to methods of absolute sterilization and ultraclean surfaces so the clones are not in any way tainted with imperfections. Such standards are extraordinary for so vast an enterprise, and Obi-Wan Kenobi is astonished.

Batches of clones are trained in an environment with exactly enough semblance of community to make them emotionally stable. Physical skills are imparted through learning devices and are perfected through practice.

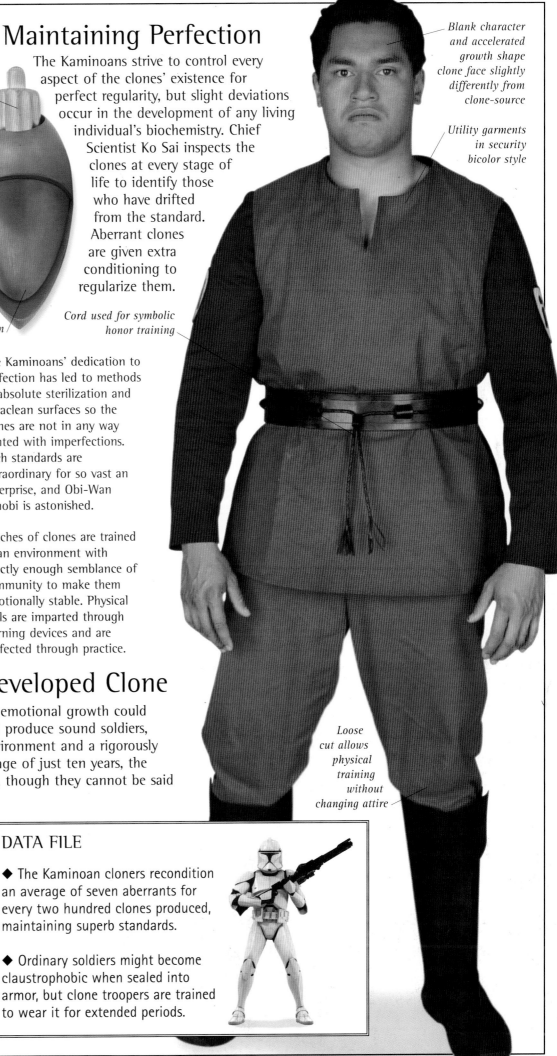

Developed Clone

The stress of accelerated physical, mental, and emotional growth could easily drive a clone insane. To counter this and produce sound soldiers, the Kaminoans provide a highly disciplined environment and a rigorously balanced development program. At a physical age of just ten years, the clones are fully developed and ready for battle, though they cannot be said to have normal personalities.

Loose cut allows physical training without changing attire

As "adults," the clone troopers resemble their source, Jango Fett. Fett lives on Kamino and helps train the troopers, knowing better than anyone how to guide their development and impart military skills to the copies of himself.

DATA FILE

◆ The Kaminoan cloners recondition an average of seven aberrants for every two hundred clones produced, maintaining superb standards.

◆ Ordinary soldiers might become claustrophobic when sealed into armor, but clone troopers are trained to wear it for extended periods.

Clone Trooper Equipment

CLONE TROOPER armor and equipment is based in part on the battle gear of the Mandalorian "shocktrooper" supercommandos, of whom Jango Fett is a survivor. Fett's light armor inspired the heavy-duty shell completely covering the clone trooper. Replacing the Mandalorian flightsuit is a pressurized black body-glove that protects against acrid vapors or even the vacuum of space. The distinctive shocktrooper "T" visor plate is adapted with an enhanced breath filter for optimal operations under the often poor environmental conditions of battle. Together with their superb training and conditioning, clone troopers feel virtually invincible with this panoply.

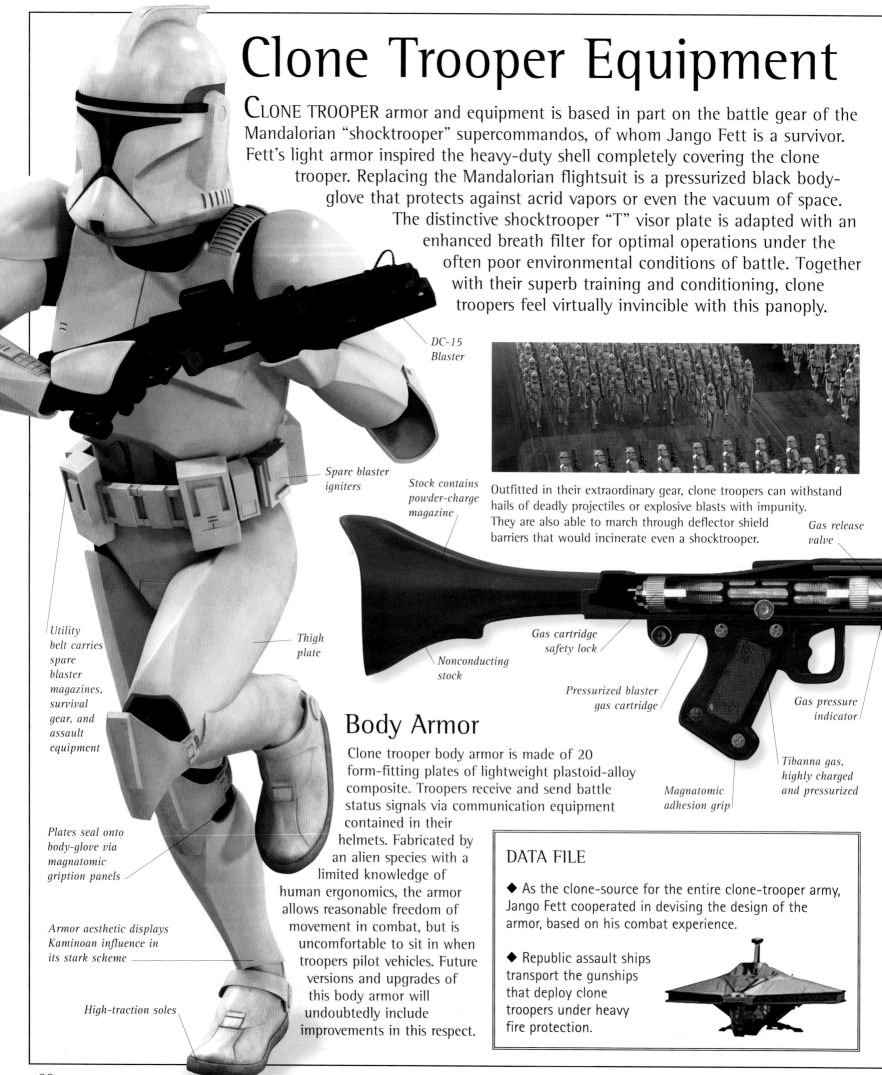

DC-15 Blaster

Spare blaster igniters

Stock contains powder-charge magazine

Outfitted in their extraordinary gear, clone troopers can withstand hails of deadly projectiles or explosive blasts with impunity. They are also able to march through deflector shield barriers that would incinerate even a shocktrooper.

Gas release valve

Thigh plate

Nonconducting stock

Gas cartridge safety lock

Utility belt carries spare blaster magazines, survival gear, and assault equipment

Pressurized blaster gas cartridge

Magnatomic adhesion grip

Gas pressure indicator

Tibanna gas, highly charged and pressurized

Body Armor

Clone trooper body armor is made of 20 form-fitting plates of lightweight plastoid-alloy composite. Troopers receive and send battle status signals via communication equipment contained in their helmets. Fabricated by an alien species with a limited knowledge of human ergonomics, the armor allows reasonable freedom of movement in combat, but is uncomfortable to sit in when troopers pilot vehicles. Future versions and upgrades of this body armor will undoubtedly include improvements in this respect.

Plates seal onto body-glove via magnatomic gription panels

Armor aesthetic displays Kaminoan influence in its stark scheme

High-traction soles

DATA FILE

◆ As the clone-source for the entire clone-trooper army, Jango Fett cooperated in devising the design of the armor, based on his combat experience.

◆ Republic assault ships transport the gunships that deploy clone troopers under heavy fire protection.

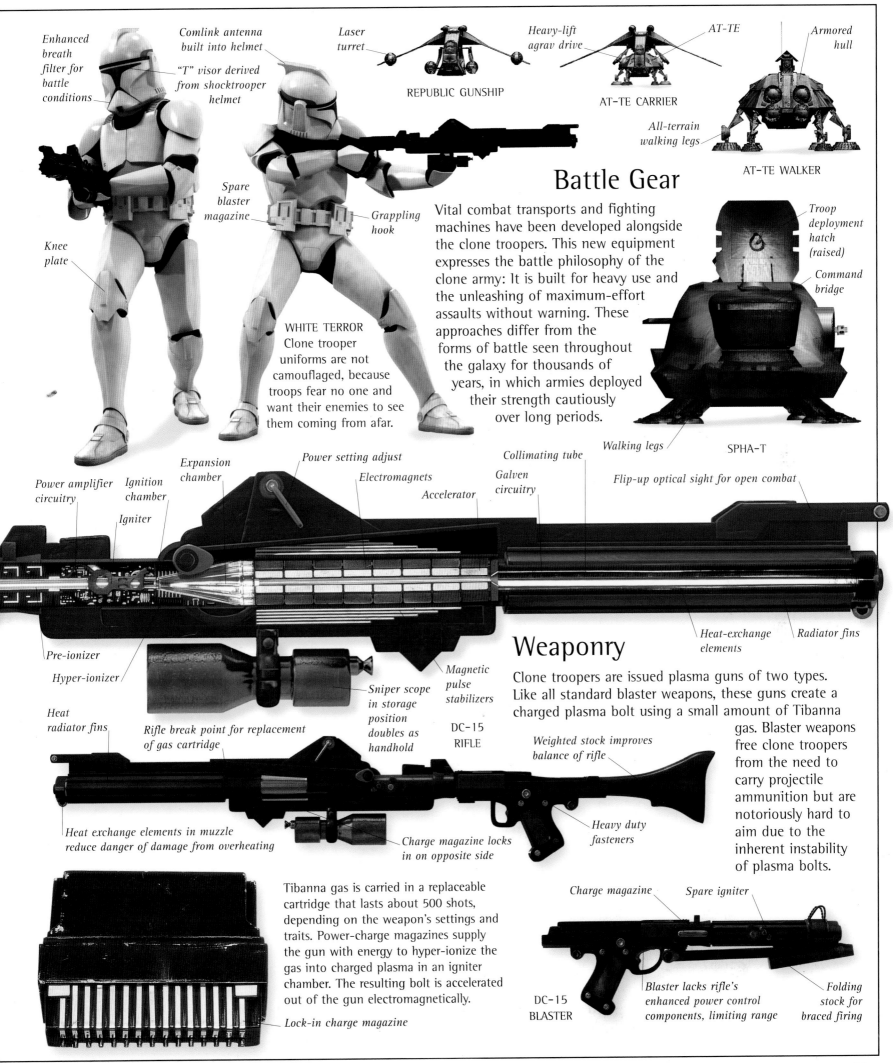

Enhanced
breath
filter for
battle
conditions

Comlink antenna
built into helmet

"T" visor derived
from shocktrooper
helmet

Laser
turret

Heavy-lift
agrav drive

AT-TE

Armored
hull

REPUBLIC GUNSHIP

AT-TE CARRIER

All-terrain
walking legs

AT-TE WALKER

Spare
blaster
magazine

Grappling
hook

Knee
plate

WHITE TERROR
Clone trooper
uniforms are not
camouflaged, because
troops fear no one and
want their enemies to see
them coming from afar.

Battle Gear

Vital combat transports and fighting
machines have been developed alongside
the clone troopers. This new equipment
expresses the battle philosophy of the
clone army: It is built for heavy use and
the unleashing of maximum-effort
assaults without warning. These
approaches differ from the
forms of battle seen throughout
the galaxy for thousands of
years, in which armies deployed
their strength cautiously
over long periods.

Troop
deployment
hatch
(raised)

Command
bridge

Walking legs

SPHA-T

Power amplifier
circuitry

Ignition
chamber

Igniter

Expansion
chamber

Power setting adjust

Electromagnets

Accelerator

Collimating tube

Galven
circuitry

Flip-up optical sight for open combat

Pre-ionizer

Hyper-ionizer

Heat
radiator fins

Rifle break point for replacement
of gas cartridge

Sniper scope
in storage
position
doubles as
handhold

Magnetic
pulse
stabilizers

DC–15
RIFLE

Heat-exchange
elements

Radiator fins

Weaponry

Clone troopers are issued plasma guns of two types.
Like all standard blaster weapons, these guns create a
charged plasma bolt using a small amount of Tibanna
gas. Blaster weapons
free clone troopers
from the need to
carry projectile
ammunition but are
notoriously hard to
aim due to the
inherent instability
of plasma bolts.

Weighted stock improves
balance of rifle

Heat exchange elements in muzzle
reduce danger of damage from overheating

Charge magazine locks
in on opposite side

Heavy duty
fasteners

Tibanna gas is carried in a replaceable
cartridge that lasts about 500 shots,
depending on the weapon's settings and
traits. Power-charge magazines supply
the gun with energy to hyper-ionize the
gas into charged plasma in an igniter
chamber. The resulting bolt is accelerated
out of the gun electromagnetically.

Lock-in charge magazine

Charge magazine

Spare igniter

DC–15
BLASTER

Blaster lacks rifle's
enhanced power control
components, limiting range

Folding
stock for
braced firing

Jango Fett–Bounty Hunter

AFTER THE MURDER of his parents, Jango Fett was adopted and raised by the legendary Mandalorian warrior army, a mercenary group who earned a reputation as the most formidable supercommandoes in the galaxy. The Jedi destroyed this dangerous force, but Fett survived and continues to wear the armored, weapon-filled uniform that helped make the Mandalorians a dreaded name. Keeping himself in top condition and training often with his equipment, Jango Fett combines physical and tactical skill with a prudent intelligence that is a rare attribute in the bounty-hunting community.

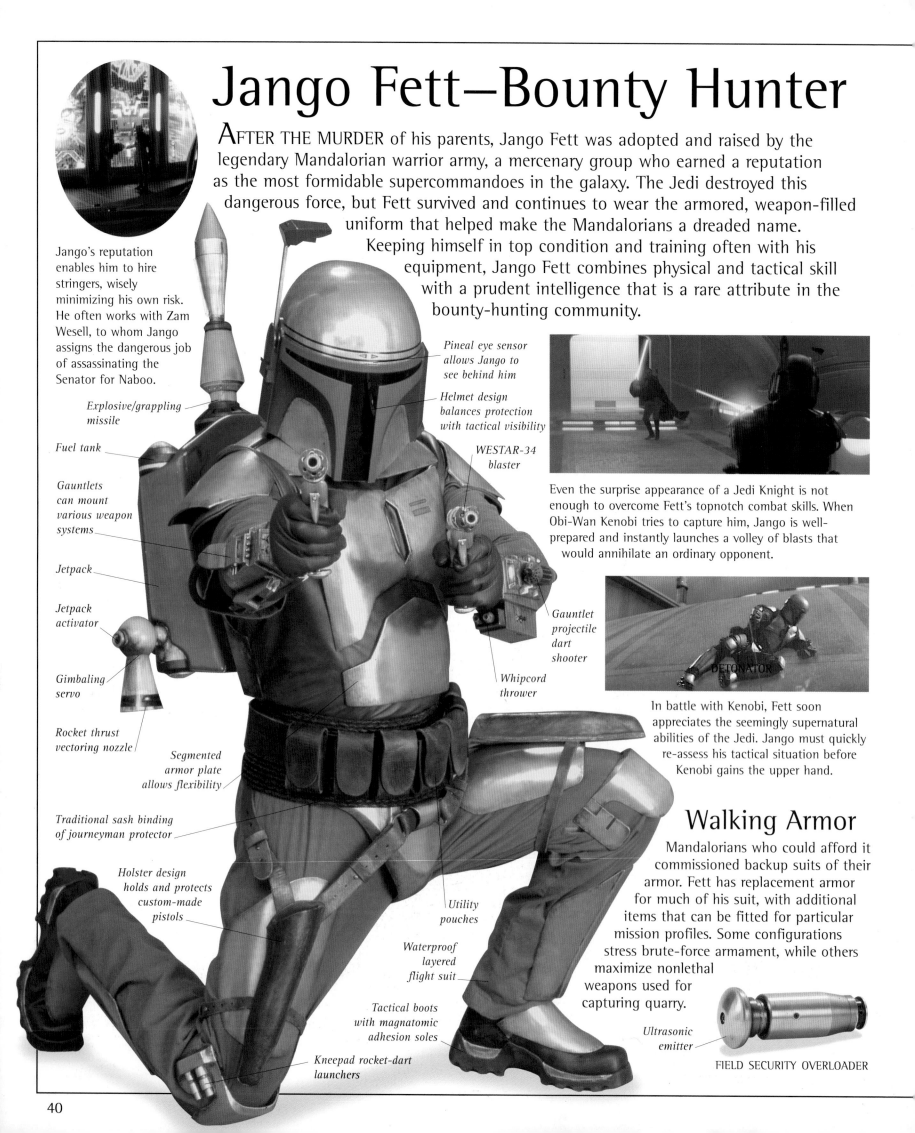

Jango's reputation enables him to hire stringers, wisely minimizing his own risk. He often works with Zam Wesell, to whom Jango assigns the dangerous job of assassinating the Senator for Naboo.

Explosive/grappling missile

Fuel tank

Gauntlets can mount various weapon systems

Jetpack

Jetpack activator

Gimbaling servo

Rocket thrust vectoring nozzle

Segmented armor plate allows flexibility

Traditional sash binding of journeyman protector

Holster design holds and protects custom-made pistols

Pineal eye sensor allows Jango to see behind him

Helmet design balances protection with tactical visibility

WESTAR-34 blaster

Gauntlet projectile dart shooter

Whipcord thrower

Utility pouches

Waterproof layered flight suit

Tactical boots with magnatomic adhesion soles

Kneepad rocket-dart launchers

Even the surprise appearance of a Jedi Knight is not enough to overcome Fett's topnotch combat skills. When Obi-Wan Kenobi tries to capture him, Jango is well-prepared and instantly launches a volley of blasts that would annihilate an ordinary opponent.

DETONATOR

In battle with Kenobi, Fett soon appreciates the seemingly supernatural abilities of the Jedi. Jango must quickly re-assess his tactical situation before Kenobi gains the upper hand.

Walking Armor

Mandalorians who could afford it commissioned backup suits of their armor. Fett has replacement armor for much of his suit, with additional items that can be fitted for particular mission profiles. Some configurations stress brute-force armament, while others maximize nonlethal weapons used for capturing quarry.

Ultrasonic emitter

FIELD SECURITY OVERLOADER

WESTAR-34 Blaster

Gas and power cell cartridge

Trigger

Weight-minimizing cutout handle

Low-power pulse indicator

Overload flash dissipator port

Favoring agility and precision over high capacity, Fett had a set of compact WESTAR-34 blasters custom-made. Designed for brief but intense surprise attacks at close range, the pistols are made of an expensive dallorian alloy, which can withstand sustained-fire heating that would melt an ordinary gun.

Code algorithm selectors

Signal projector

Activator

LOCK BREAKER

Targeting rangefinder swings down for sighting

Mandalorian helmet

Concussion missile

Never governed by passions or panic, Fett coolly calculates his every move, always playing to win or survive. He knows when to make use of evasion and thus outlasts both rivals and opponents.

Secondary jetpack

Warhead missile

Blades deploy from gauntlet for surprise in unarmed combat

Energized blast dissipation vest

Realizing that Kenobi is a formidable opponent, Fett launches his jetpack missile set for explosive charge. The missile can be optionally locked dead as a grappling hook. Set to explode, it would kill any ordinary humanoid, but will it kill a Jedi?

Holstered WESTAR-34 blaster

Missile thrust vent

JETPACKS
Fett's gear includes two models of jetpack, one more heavily armored and carrying a larger-bore missile.

DATA FILE

◆ Ten years ago, Darth Tyranus recruited Jango as the clone-source for the Kaminoans' secret clone-army project.

◆ Jango's Mandalorian armor is one of the only surviving sets of this feared and elusive panoply.

Professional

Raised in a brutal frontier environment on Concord Dawn, Fett is tough and self-reliant. He has worked out his own sense of morality which is honorable by his standards. He keeps his bargains and he earns his pay. As a bounty hunter, Fett has become so professionally formidable that planetary governments are known to hire him.

Fine-bore missile

Missile targeting rangefinder

Missile charge boost

Jango and Boba Fett

ENTRY KEYPAD

THE MANDALORIAN WAY lives on in the bond between Jango Fett and his son Boba. Growing up at his father's side, Boba has learned the value of superior training, judgement, and weaponry. To Boba, Jango stands above the greed and betrayal encountered in the underworld, and is a man of honor who is unfailingly truthful with him. To young Boba, Jango Fett is father, family, ideal, and hero, the greatest of the Mandalorians and the image of his own destiny.

Jango maintains a Spartan apartment on Kamino. He uses it as a safe house for himself and his son, far from the dangerous entanglements of his professional life.

Earpiece receives signals from Slave I and protects Jango from enemy sonic weapons

Jango teaches Boba by example

Bicolor tunic in traditional security style

Practiced fighting stance

Utility pouches

Like Father, Like Son

In Mandalorian tradition, fathers were responsible for training their sons in combat skills. At age 13, boys had to face the trials of manhood. Although these rites could be fatal, actual deaths were extremely rare because candidates were so well prepared. The close father-son bond, built on respect, trust, and discipline, produced highly capable and confident individuals.

Lamp creates apparently sourceless light

Decorative frame

SETLA LAMP

Tone activator

Illuminator

KAMINOAN DOORBELL

Monangular screen

Charge plate

PERSONAL DATAPAD
Jango uses portable computer systems to store mission information. They are programmed to erase all stored information if not handled correctly.

Military-grade cloth pants

Mandalorian youth boots

Armored kneepad

Shinplate

Reinforced boot

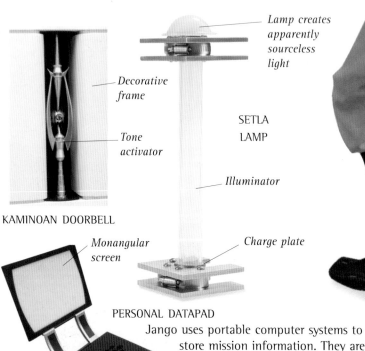

Boba Fett

Young Boba Fett is perceptive and intelligent. He has learned to assess situations carefully, and to listen more than he talks. When Obi-Wan Kenobi appears at the Fetts' apartment, Boba immediately senses trouble, but betrays none of his concern.

Disciplined posture

Rain cloak

Jango teaches Boba to be self-reliant and to trust his skills. He also trains the boy to handle dangerous bounty hunting equipment. Exotic armor and advanced starship systems are commonplace elements in Boba's daily life.

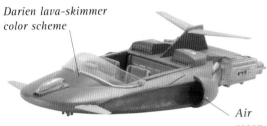

Darien lava-skimmer color scheme

BOBA'S AIRSPEEDER MODEL

Air scoop

Jango's stored armor

Oovo security force markings

Systems status readouts

SLAVE I READOUT

Energy shield generator

Large, variable-opacity windshield allows superb range of vision

Wing rotation axis

Repulsorlift wing

Wing extension struts

Boba knows when to stay in the background. Jango trusts his son's discretion and keeps him around even during critical meetings.

Main hatch

Boarding ramp

Target scanner (under outer plating)

Missile launcher

DATA FILE

◆ Boba Fett is a perfect, unaltered clone of his father, part of Jango's compensation from the Kaminoans.

◆ Jango knows that Darth Tyranus, who recruited him for the clone-army project, is actually the Separatist leader, Count Dooku.

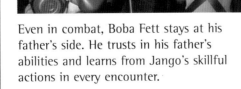

Even in combat, Boba Fett stays at his father's side. He trusts in his father's abilities and learns from Jango's skillful actions in every encounter.

Slave I

Jango Fett pilots a prototype Kuat Systems *Firespray*-class interceptor of the kind made for patrolling the prison planet of Oovo IV. Fett reasoned that a starship designed to thwart some of the galaxy's most hardened criminals would be excellent for his unusual line of work.

Charge balance readout

WEAPONS MONITOR

The Lars Family

Settler's simple hairstyle

Rough clothing made in Anchorhead

Tunic

Desert robe

MUSHROOM JAR

TATOOINE'S moisture farmers survive in territories most other people consider uninhabitable. In their search for an independent existence away from the overcrowding and often slave-like employments of the Core Worlds, the Lars family have made Tatooine's barren desert their home. Rendered close-knit by the dangers and hardships they all face, the Lars family and the moisture-farming community band together against the native Tusken Raiders. Pioneer settler Cliegg Lars earned his farm by a homestead claim, raising his son Owen on the great salt flats, together with his second wife, a former slave named Shmi Skywalker.

Moisture farms on the salt flats of Tatooine use arrays of vaporator towers spread out across vast distances to extract minute amounts of water from the atmosphere. A precious commodity on the desert world, water can be used for barter, for sale, or for hydroponic gardens. Homesteads are dug into the ground to provide respite from extreme temperatures.

Owen and Beru

The small town of Anchorhead provides a nexus for the moisture-farming community of the Great Chott salt flat. There, Owen Lars met Beru Whitesun, his girlfriend. Beru's family have been moisture farmers for three generations, making them among the settlers most thoroughly adapted to Tatooine life.

Owen never expected to meet his step-brother, Anakin, knowing that Jedi must sever their family ties. When Anakin arrives, Owen has mixed feelings about his more worldly relation who left his own mother to become a Jedi.

The Lars' kitchen is a simple, functional space built around the basic concern of conserving moisture. Food is never left out for long, and moisture traps are built into the self-sealing cabinets.

DATA FILE

◆ Owen Lars was born to Cliegg Lars and his first wife Aika before Cliegg left the Core World of Ator.

◆ The Lars family maintains an array of some 63 water vaporators spread out across the flat desert around the homestead, making their farm a relatively small one by Tatooine standards.

C-3PO

Anakin Skywalker built the working skeleton of C-3PO out of scrounged droid parts when he was just a boy and still a slave. Two years after her son's departure, Shmi Skywalker acquired a set of old droid plating from her then master, Watto. Shmi installed the plates to help the droid last longer in the sandy environment.

Enhanced vision spots circuitry damage

Sub-par droid plating

Flexible unplated midsection

Power and impulse wiring

Mostly sandproof joint

Cliegg Lars

Cliegg Lars left behind life in a cramped garret within a centuries-old Core World skyscraper to run a farm on Tatooine. Looking for a farmhand, instead he found a woman whom he fell in love with. In order to marry Shmi, he bought her freedom from Watto, the junk dealer.

Improvised protective gear

Most settlers have no blasters

When Shmi Skywalker is kidnapped by Tusken Raiders, a posse of moisture farmers go in search of her. But these peaceable folk are little prepared to face the savagery of Tusken Raiders.

Mechno-Chair

When Tusken Raiders ambush the nearly defenseless settlers who attempt to rescue Shmi, Cliegg Lars' leg is cut off by a lethal trick-wire. Refusing to be fitted with a mechno-leg, Cliegg is confined to a power chair.

Salvaged metal from transport container

Control stick

Activator

Power unit

Repulsor coils

Induction drives

Footrest

Overheat radiators

Homemade blaster

Power cell

Discarded ignition chamber

Simple laser sight

SETTLER WEAPONS
The few weapons available to the impoverished settlers are low-powered blasters.

Stun blast nozzle

Facing Loss

After the Tusken tragedy, some wonder whether the moisture farming community will be abandoned. With the death of Shmi, Cliegg Lars has lost as much as anyone, yet he remains determined to live out the life he has worked so hard to create.

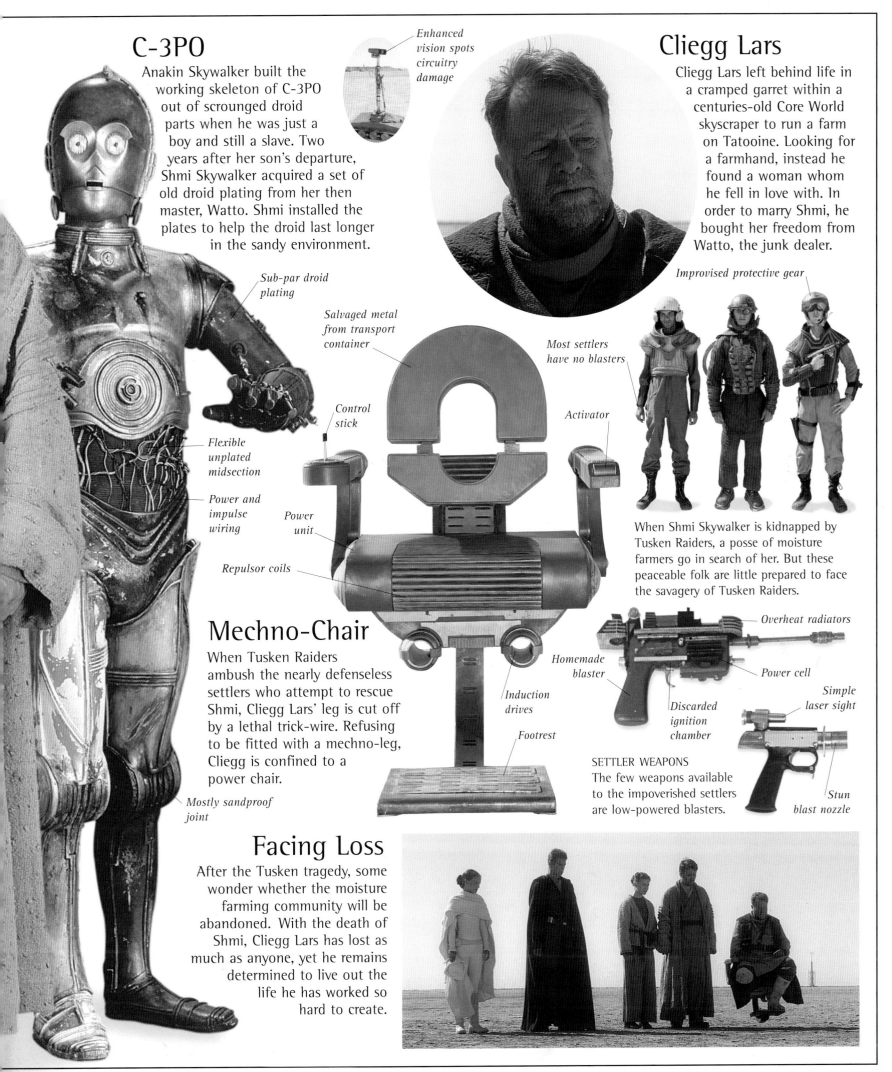

Eyeslit

Sandshroud

Tusken Raiders

Tᴀᴛᴏᴏɪɴᴇ'ꜱ ɴᴀᴛɪᴠᴇ Tusken Raiders, or Sand People, are violent enemies of the moisture farmers, with whom they compete for precious water sources on the desert planet. These fearsome creatures are often larger than humans yet they blend into the landscape with baffling ease, allowing them to move almost invisibly. Sand People live in tribal clans loosely scattered across the dunes and canyonlands of Tatooine. They travel lightly and possess few objects, the most treasured of which are the skulls of their ancestors and krayt dragon pearls.

Sand People are reputed to slay anyone foolish enough to come near their sacred wells.

Jewelry made of metal taken from slain captives

Female Tusken's pouch

Sand People live in Tatooine's most barren wastes, where no human settlers could survive. For most of the year, Tusken Raiders rove the desert, but during the height of the hot season, many tribes live in semi-permanent camps.

Womp-rat tusks

Even hands must always be covered

Only someone with the powers of a Jedi could enter a Tusken camp unnoticed. Sand People are uncannily skilled sentries, and can detect humans entering their territory long before they themselves are seen by the intruders.

Desert cloak

DATA FILE

◆ Many gruesome legends surround Tusken Raiders, who are even known to spit streams of blood at their victims during attacks.

◆ Sand People fashion spirit masks from natural materials for use in rituals.

Shrouded In Mystery

Tusken Raiders are strongly divided along gender lines. Females maintain the camps while the males hunt and fight. Sand People keep their flesh carefully covered, only revealing it on their wedding night. For any other exposure of skin, even accidental, Tusken Raiders are banished or killed, depending on the tribe.

Bandaged feet

Gaffi stick

Sandbat venom

Simple charged-projectile rifle for long-distance shooting

Blood spitter

Ammo pouches

Typical double-axe

Sand Gear

Throughout their desert range, Sand People wear similar gear, although each tribal clan has its own distinctive details. Some groups wear a kind of sand-repelling capsule around their necks, while others use simple scarves. Raiders reject most advanced technology, but will take horrific advantage of a stolen blaster gun until its power is spent.

WARNING POSE

Tools and rations

Krayt dragon horn

GADERFFI
The Sand People's traditional weapon is the gaderffi, or "gaffi" stick. These dreaded axes are made from krayt dragon horn and spacecraft plating salvaged from desert wrecks.

Tusken Raiders can hide even in the featureless landscape of the salt flats, where they sometimes lie in wait to kidnap or kill moisture farmers who come out to tend their vaporators.

Unisex youth helmet

Eye and mouth slit

Full-length sandshroud

Tusken Uli-ah

Sand People children, called Uli-ah, wear unisex garments that hide all flesh. These traditional clothes protect Uli-ah from sun, sand, and wind, and conserve precious moisture. Young Tusken Raiders lack full tribal acceptance until they complete a rite of passage at age 15.

Sandcloak

Sand People make a few basic items such as stoves from scavenged and stolen metal. More complex devices are usually taboo.

Ancient wood poles

Skin covering hardened for use at seasonal camp

Tent carried on bantha for travel

Spiked club

Carryall pouch

Entry forbidden to non-family

URTYA TENT
Sand People travel with light tents called urtya. These dwellings are made from skins, tendons, and sticks gathered from occasional exposures of Tatooine's sand-flooded, long-dead forests.

Urtah (Tusken Raider carrying pack)

Sacred ancestor skulls kept inside

Hardener made from bantha spittle

Sandrobe

In the droid foundries of Geonosis, the Count hopes to have found the anvil upon which he can forge the sword of the Republic's undoing.

Count's gaze immobilizes weak-minded individuals

Count Dooku

THE DANGEROUS AND ELEGANT Count Dooku was once a Jedi Master of great repute. He left the Jedi Order after the Battle of Naboo, returning to his homeworld of Serenno and his family title of Count. By protesting the failure of galactic government, Dooku has swayed many systems to the Separatist movement, which seeks independence from the Republic, but his real motives lurk in darkness. The Count has always wielded considerable power—by natural authority, by lightsaber, and now by wealth and persuasion. This double-dealing master of the Force has taken a place at the heart of galactic events and he threatens the very survival of the Republic.

Cape is emblem of Count of Serenno

Curved lightsaber hilt allows precise crossparry moves

Cape enlarges Count's silhouette to intimidating effect

Dark Alignment

Although Dooku joined the Order at the usual age, he never fully gave it his inmost allegiance. He maintained a streak of independence, which he transmitted to his pupils, including the late Qui-Gon Jinn. Dooku's considerable strength in the Force made him enigmatic even to Yoda, and there were whispers that he experimented with Sith teachings, using a dark Holocron kept in the Jedi Archives. The Council underestimated Dooku's interest in power.

Underlayer made of costly, fine-grade armorweave fabric, which drapes like silk and helps dissipate blast or lightsaber energy

Elegant, tall dress boots

DATA FILE

◆ The Count is master of his family's fortune and one of the wealthiest men in the galaxy. He could field an army on his own resources.

◆ Dooku's teacher was Yoda. The great Jedi Master hoped, with careful teaching, to overcome the effects of Dooku's persistent independent spirit.

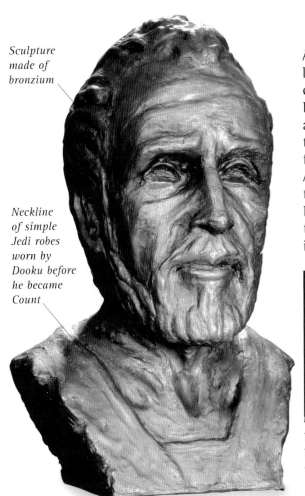

Sculpture made of bronzium

Neckline of simple Jedi robes worn by Dooku before he became Count

Dooku's Lightsaber

As a Jedi Master, Count Dooku set aside the lightsaber he built as a young Padawan and created a superior one, as Jedi sometimes do. In creating his personalized design, he chose a configuration that had no connection to that of his master, Yoda, nor to the style in fashion at the time. Instead, he studied Jedi Archives records to create a lightsaber of the type that was standard in the heyday of Form II lightsaber combat. Form II is an ancient technique that favors long, elegant moves and incredible deftness of hand.

Emitter guard

Thumb trigger can shorten blade instantly for short-range surprise attack

Blade emitter

Inclined blade focusing chamber

Thermal radiator grooves

Dooku tempts the captured Obi-Wan Kenobi with an offer to join him in the Separatist movement. The Count subtly uses the Force to probe Obi-Wan's spirit for inner weaknesses.

Sith synthetic crystals (inside saber) replace original ones for greater power

The Lost Twenty

Only 20 individuals in the history of the Jedi Order have ever renounced their commissions. Their leave-taking is sorely felt among the Jedi, who memorialize them with portrait busts in the Archives. Count Dooku is the most recent of the "lost" ones. He is considered the most bitter loss because the Force was so strong in him.

The curved hilt of Dooku's lightsaber allows for superior finesse and precise blade control. This design gives Dooku an edge when facing Jedi, who have mostly trained to use lightsabers to deflect blaster bolts.

Projector

Cells given by Sith Master

HOLOPROJECTOR
After he left the Jedi Order, Dooku was no longer able to use the Sith Holocron in the Archives. He now studies holographic cells containing mystic teachings of shadowy power.

When the arrival of the Jedi forces spoils his primary plans, Dooku uses one of his several means of escape—a small, open-cockpit speeder bike.

Activator

Fastener

Magnatomic adhesion plates

Dooku reveals the full measure of his dark nature when he casts legendary Sith lightning. Virtually impossible to deflect, Sith lightning causes excruciating pain and weakens life. The Jedi possess no exact equivalent to such an evil use of the Force.

Compound power cell

Reserve power cell

Phase A power cell

The Separatists

COUNT DOOKU'S CALL for independence from the decaying and increasingly corrupt Republic is answered by some of the most significant and authoritative factions in the galaxy. Among them stands a sinister gathering of commercial empires and megaconglomerates, whose power could rival that of the Republic itself. Disaffected and opportunistic Senators also support the Separatist movement. The political system was never constructed to deal with the rise of corporate superpowers, whose motives and morals focus on profit alone. Without decisive support from the Galactic Senate, the Republic's very structure is in danger of being undermined.

The Corporate Alliance

The Corporate Alliance is the negotiating body for the galaxy's major commercial operations. As head of the largest corporation, Passel Argente commands the office of Alliance Magistrate. Argente has risen to great heights of wealth and power as chairman of the merchandising conglomerate called Lethe. Workers and consumers are encouraged to identify with the company in a near-religious way.

GILRAMOS LIBKATH

Large, pompous miter

Conniving gesture

NUTE GUNRAY

Elaborate Neimoidian headdress

Oath-taking gesture

Sign of insincerity

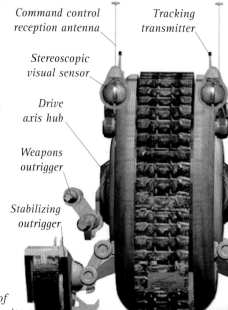

Command control reception antenna

Tracking transmitter

Stereoscopic visual sensor

Drive axis hub

Weapons outrigger

Stabilizing outrigger

Drive axis hub

High-traction drive tread

Robust male cranial horn

PASSEL ARGENTE

Oily cloak

CORPORATE ALLIANCE TANK DROID
When Alliance corporations face resistance to their development plans, Tank Droids are used to clear the way. The wheel-like machines are widely feared.

Grasping hands

The Trade Federation

The Trade Federation controls freighters, ports, and way stations on the galactic commerce routes. Its power is profitably supported by a droid army, which operates under the guise of "securing the lines of trade." Trade officials appear immune to prosecution for their brutal intimidation.

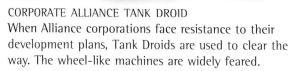

Communications tower

TRADE FEDERATION CORE SHIP
Large Trade Federation freighters are not designed for planetary landings. However, the core ships can detach from the freighters and descend on their own.

The Commerce Guild

The Commerce Guild seeks to control any large corporation involved in raw materials. Increasingly, it enforces tribute payments with its private army. The Guild maximizes profit by stifling alternative technologies and bribing corrupt officials and Senators to control market forces with tariffs.

Traditional skullcap

Gossam rings elongate neck

PRESIDENT SHU MAI

HOMING SPIDER DROID

Armored body core

Extension hydraulics

All-terrain legs

Gracile female cranial horn

Homing laser

Parallax signal tracing dish

Koorivan matron's hood

Ambulation motors

DENARIA KEE (AIDE)

Tracing antenna

Infrared photoreceptor

Formal breastplate of office

DWARF SPIDER DROID
Commerce Guild army droids are built with striding legs for roadless terrain on rugged mining worlds. These destructive droids hunt down operations attempting to evade tribute payments.

Subservient gesture

Robe made of shimmerbird tongues

The IG Banking Clan

The InterGalactic Banking Clan is headquartered on Muunilinst. It is vastly powerful, with most influence shared by a few old banking families. The fiscally prudent chairman San Hill views the galaxy in purely monetary terms, so he naturally finances both sides of a major conflict.

Pale skin from indoor living

Palo Banking garb

SAN HILL

Hailfire missile launcher pods

Hoop wheel

HAILFIRE DROID
Hailfire Droids roll rapidly into action to discourage those who might default on IG Banking Clan loans. Murderous explosive missile launchers dispatch "late payment notices."

Cyclopean photoreceptor

Sequenced magpulse drive

PO NUDO

AIDE

Shi'ido changeling in disguise

TIKKES

Large aural chamber

Food manipulation tentacles

Senators

Demoralized by bureaucratic inaction and corruption, some Senators see Count Dooku's bid for independence as a brave and noble cause. Others align themselves with the Separatists merely for greater personal gain.

DATA FILE

◆ Count Dooku leads the Separatists and knows every faction's weak points.

◆ Most commercial armies are legally licensed even though they violate the spirit of the laws against private armies.

Geonosian Aristocracy

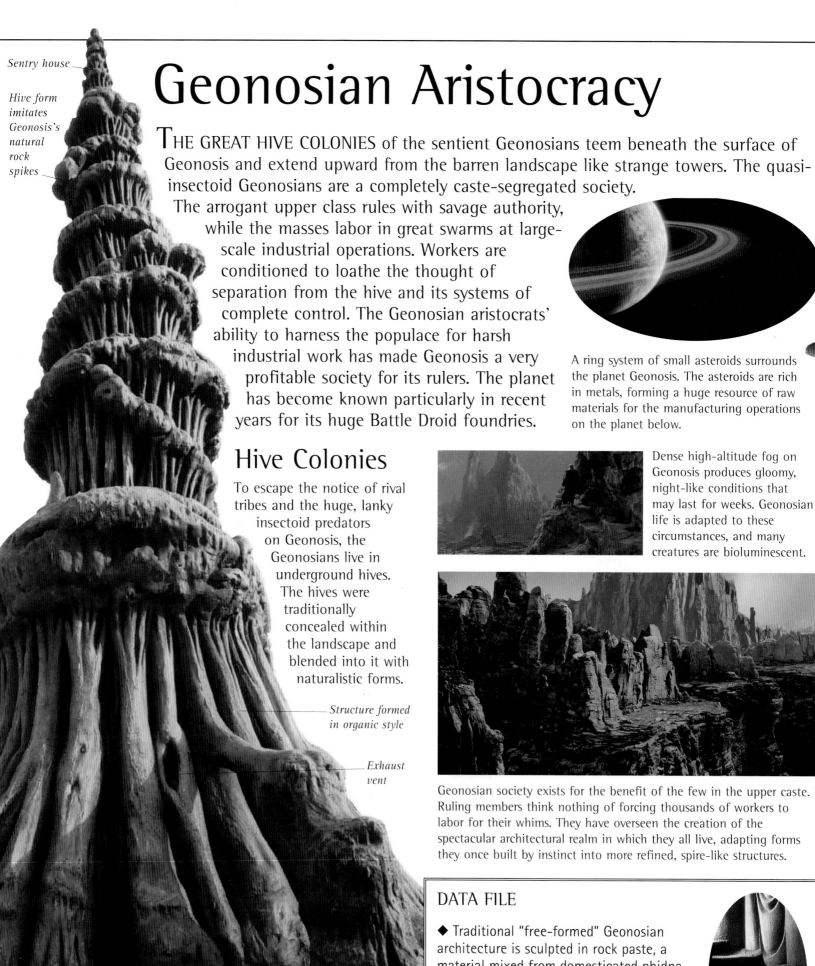

Sentry house

Hive form imitates Geonosis's natural rock spikes

THE GREAT HIVE COLONIES of the sentient Geonosians teem beneath the surface of Geonosis and extend upward from the barren landscape like strange towers. The quasi-insectoid Geonosians are a completely caste-segregated society. The arrogant upper class rules with savage authority, while the masses labor in great swarms at large-scale industrial operations. Workers are conditioned to loathe the thought of separation from the hive and its systems of complete control. The Geonosian aristocrats' ability to harness the populace for harsh industrial work has made Geonosis a very profitable society for its rulers. The planet has become known particularly in recent years for its huge Battle Droid foundries.

A ring system of small asteroids surrounds the planet Geonosis. The asteroids are rich in metals, forming a huge resource of raw materials for the manufacturing operations on the planet below.

Hive Colonies

To escape the notice of rival tribes and the huge, lanky insectoid predators on Geonosis, the Geonosians live in underground hives. The hives were traditionally concealed within the landscape and blended into it with naturalistic forms.

Structure formed in organic style

Exhaust vent

Dense high-altitude fog on Geonosis produces gloomy, night-like conditions that may last for weeks. Geonosian life is adapted to these circumstances, and many creatures are bioluminescent.

Geonosian society exists for the benefit of the few in the upper caste. Ruling members think nothing of forcing thousands of workers to labor for their whims. They have overseen the creation of the spectacular architectural realm in which they all live, adapting forms they once built by instinct into more refined, spire-like structures.

DATA FILE

◆ Traditional "free-formed" Geonosian architecture is sculpted in rock paste, a material mixed from domesticated phidna parasite excretions and stone powders.

◆ Geonosian phidna are cultivated in hydroponic gardens to supply the hive construction industry.

Sun Fac

Upper-caste wings

Poggle's chief lieutenant, Sun Fac, ensures that his master's will is done throughout Geonosis. Unusually intelligent and creative for a Geonosian, Sun Fac is adept at playing whatever role will best accomplish the needs of the moment. He may be a sympathetic listener or a heartless executioner, depending on which will increase productivity.

Poggle the Lesser

The Stalgasin hive colony ruled by Archduke Poggle the Lesser currently controls all the other major hives on Geonosis. Poggle has negotiated with outworld interests and coordinated widespread planetary hive efforts on the largest industrial projects ever undertaken by Geonosian society—the building of colossal numbers of Battle Droids for the Trade Federation and their Separatist allies. The tremendous income from these projects has secured Poggle's power, but this situation could change, as it has done in the past. The infighting rife in Geonosian society usually makes clients reluctant to place large orders.

Spider emblem of office

Long wattles favored by high-caste Geonosians

Trappings of aristocracy

Expensive visgura thread made from extinct cave spider's giant egg cases

Wings not used after youth

Bracelets represent number of prime hives under Poggle's control

Command staff

Additional pair of antlers grow each standard year

Armored hide

Exoskeletal flexibility joint

Sharpened tip used to prod inferiors

Blade-like images are common in Geonosian art, reflecting the violence of Geonosian society. Poggle is rumored to have had his political opponent murdered in a coup and to carry the rival's limb bones as a staff.

Toe structure allows Geonosians to cling to rock crags

Common on both Geonosis and neighboring Tatooine, massifs are emblems of authority for Geonosian aristrocrats, who keep them as pets. Massifs also rid the hives of vermin in return for safety from predators outside.

53

Trade Federation Battle Droids

THE WEALTHY TRADE FEDERATION is a key faction in the Separatist movement, supplying its army of Battle Droids. The Trade Federation's defeat in the Battle of Naboo made clear the need for stronger, more independent infantry forces, and thus the Super Battle Droids were commissioned as improvements on their standard, skeletal-form predecessors. Like the terrifying droideka, these military-grade robots violate Republic regulations on private security forces, but the Neimoidians have too much influence to fear the galactic courts. Count Dooku himself arranged the deal in which a large force of Super Battle Droids are being secretly manufactured within the droid foundries of Geonosis, building even greater power for the Separatists.

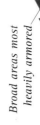

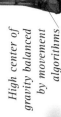

Neimoidians are too fearful to fight their own battles and too deceitful to trust living soldiers, preferring to use Battle Droids for their nefarious purposes. Often criticized for their cowardliness, they have found Count Dooku surprisingly supportive of their mechanized army.

Broad areas most heavily armored

Dehumanized silhouette increases intimidation effect

Limbs remain narrow in forward silhouette for target minimization

High center of gravity balanced by movement algorithms

Enhanced signal receptor package

Thick acertron armor protects primary power unit in chest

Super Battle Droid

The tough and durable Super Battle Droid's armor and reinforced joints sacrifice some mobility for improved protection. For economy, the design makes use of standard Battle Droid internal components, but packages them in a much stronger shell.

Flexible armored midsection

Cryogenically-tempered body-shell elements are hardened, but flex slightly under stress to reduce breakage

Main signal receptor unit buried in reinforced armor

Arms stronger than Battle Droid limbs

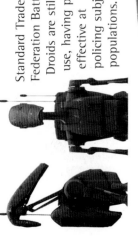

Standard Trade Federation Battle Droids are still in use, having proven effective at policing subject populations.

Heavy shoulder armor protects command signal receptor

Heavy droideka can project its own defensive shield

Complex form can fold up into a ball shape for movement to battle site

Custom-made blaster units use high-pressure blaster gas

Handtip contains firing impulse transmitter to trigger standard blaster weapons

Blaster hands built only for battle

Droideka

Heavy-duty droidekas are invulnerable to standard blaster weapons and Jedi lightsabers. These fearsome and illegal assault robots have been known to blast even their owners if not perfectly operated. Neimoidian lawyers have helped the Colicoid manufacturers of the droideka evade costly death and damage lawsuits.

Recess on hidden inner surface to reduce weight

High-torque motors

Firing impulse generators

Excess heat radiated through calf vanes

Shinplate hard-forged in one piece

Reinforced ankle joint

Strap-on foot tips can be replaced with claws or pads suited to different terrain

Monogrip hands lack dexterity but are hard to damage

Knee joint bearings hermetically sealed

Geonosian Drones

LEGIONS OF DRONES serve the Geonosian aristocracy and live within the rigid dictates of hive society. The three biologically distinct castes of drones have been further altered by genetic modification and selective breeding to produce drones specialized for many roles inside the hive. Drones have few rights, limited exercise of free will, and are executed with little concern if they prove aberrant, as there are always more to take their place. For the average drone, with its limited mentality, such a life of communal work is the only one it would want.

Drones have no rooms, possessions, or personal space of their own. To conserve resources for Geonosian rulers, drones may be ordered into sleep-like stasis when they are not needed, reducing their requirements for food and space.

Geonosian sentries stand guard against hive invaders, which may be large verminous creatures or drones from rival hives. Geonosian intruders may be seeking to raid them, sabotage their works, or shift the balance of power by assassinating rulers.

BINDERS WORN BY CAPTIVES

Charged tip delivers shock

Insulated grip

Pulse lock points weld hasp tight

Electronic release mechanism

Rather than sacrifice hive resources to support prisoners, Geonosians make captives serve as public entertainment in the arena, where they are subjected to combat against vicious beasts or each other. These entertainments reinforce the power of Geonosian rulers and pacify the drone masses with violence.

Vestigial wings of service drone

Tether tie-offs

Saddle horn provides grip for rider

Saddle rig

Rim beading decoration

Tail stinger amputated

Strong neck vertebrae carry heavy head

Small braincase of drone

Elongated snout for digging into egg caches

Drone harness styles vary little

Picador

The picadors control the creatures and criminals in the arena. The position is one of the few of note to which a drone can aspire. Drones of any caste may become picadors if they prove themselves in the arena, after which they are allowed to learn the work of goading beasts and removing bodies.

Blunt teeth for mashing eggs

ORRAYS
Tame orrays carry picadors in the arena. In antiquity, orrays hunted for the mass deposits of Geonosian eggs laid to start a new hive, devouring thousands of larvae in a single meal.

Anodized staff

STATIC PIKE

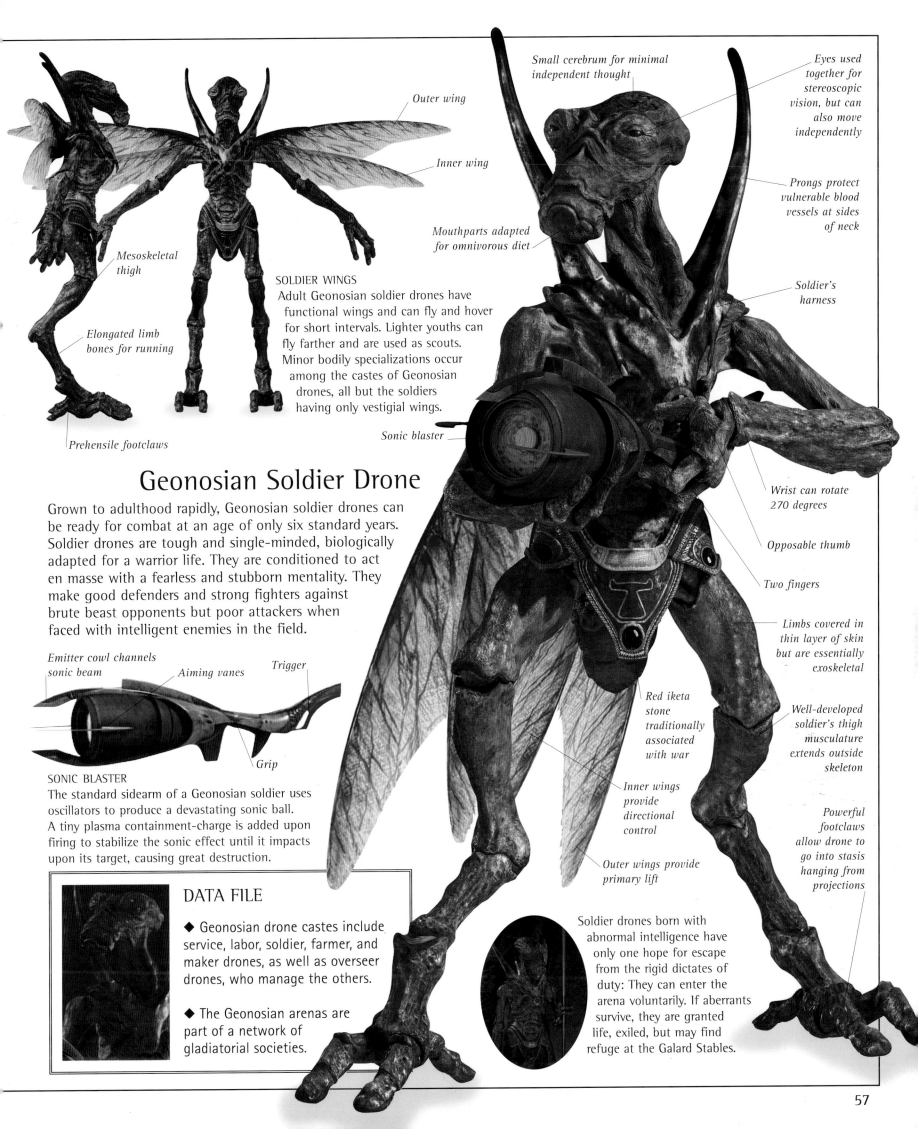

Outer wing

Inner wing

Mesoskeletal thigh

Elongated limb bones for running

Prehensile footclaws

SOLDIER WINGS
Adult Geonosian soldier drones have functional wings and can fly and hover for short intervals. Lighter youths can fly farther and are used as scouts. Minor bodily specializations occur among the castes of Geonosian drones, all but the soldiers having only vestigial wings.

Small cerebrum for minimal independent thought

Eyes used together for stereoscopic vision, but can also move independently

Prongs protect vulnerable blood vessels at sides of neck

Mouthparts adapted for omnivorous diet

Soldier's harness

Sonic blaster

Wrist can rotate 270 degrees

Opposable thumb

Two fingers

Limbs covered in thin layer of skin but are essentially exoskeletal

Geonosian Soldier Drone

Grown to adulthood rapidly, Geonosian soldier drones can be ready for combat at an age of only six standard years. Soldier drones are tough and single-minded, biologically adapted for a warrior life. They are conditioned to act en masse with a fearless and stubborn mentality. They make good defenders and strong fighters against brute beast opponents but poor attackers when faced with intelligent enemies in the field.

Emitter cowl channels sonic beam

Aiming vanes

Trigger

Grip

Red iketa stone traditionally associated with war

Well-developed soldier's thigh musculature extends outside skeleton

SONIC BLASTER
The standard sidearm of a Geonosian soldier uses oscillators to produce a devastating sonic ball. A tiny plasma containment-charge is added upon firing to stabilize the sonic effect until it impacts upon its target, causing great destruction.

Inner wings provide directional control

Outer wings provide primary lift

Powerful footclaws allow drone to go into stasis hanging from projections

DATA FILE

◆ Geonosian drone castes include service, labor, soldier, farmer, and maker drones, as well as overseer drones, who manage the others.

◆ The Geonosian arenas are part of a network of gladiatorial societies.

Soldier drones born with abnormal intelligence have only one hope for escape from the rigid dictates of duty: They can enter the arena voluntarily. If aberrants survive, they are granted life, exiled, but may find refuge at the Galard Stables.

Arena Beasts

CONDEMNED PRISONERS and gladiators face a terrifying array of monsters in the Geonosian arenas. Common criminals are strung up or let loose with the beasts, which are released from underground hive pens. Many of these creatures behave in predictably gruesome and crowd-pleasing ways, and some are trained by their keepers to maximize their more hideous behaviors. The most crowd-pleasing spectacle is saved for last, when rare beasts from far-flung star systems are released into the arena to savage criminals deserving of special attention.

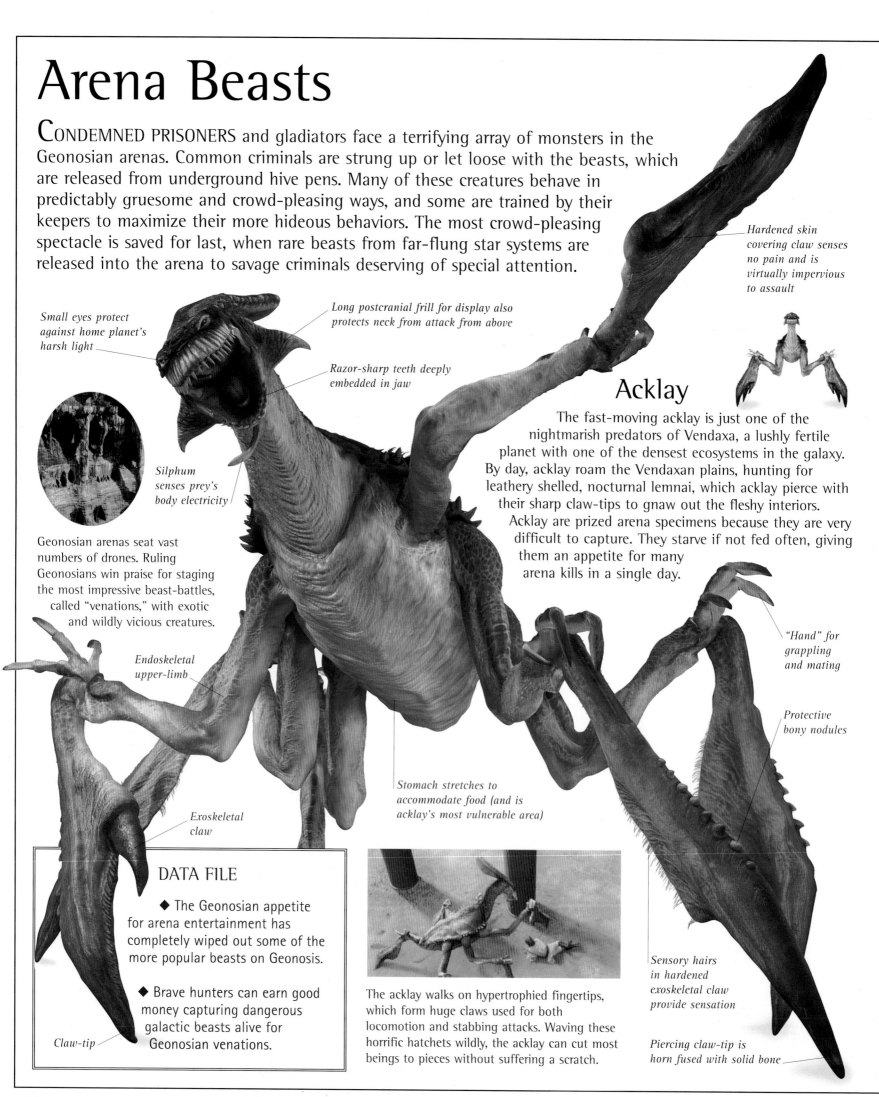

Hardened skin covering claw senses no pain and is virtually impervious to assault

Small eyes protect against home planet's harsh light

Long postcranial frill for display also protects neck from attack from above

Razor-sharp teeth deeply embedded in jaw

Acklay

The fast-moving acklay is just one of the nightmarish predators of Vendaxa, a lushly fertile planet with one of the densest ecosystems in the galaxy. By day, acklay roam the Vendaxan plains, hunting for leathery shelled, nocturnal lemnai, which acklay pierce with their sharp claw-tips to gnaw out the fleshy interiors. Acklay are prized arena specimens because they are very difficult to capture. They starve if not fed often, giving them an appetite for many arena kills in a single day.

Silphum senses prey's body electricity

Geonosian arenas seat vast numbers of drones. Ruling Geonosians win praise for staging the most impressive beast-battles, called "venations," with exotic and wildly vicious creatures.

"Hand" for grappling and mating

Endoskeletal upper-limb

Protective bony nodules

Exoskeletal claw

Stomach stretches to accommodate food (and is acklay's most vulnerable area)

DATA FILE

◆ The Geonosian appetite for arena entertainment has completely wiped out some of the more popular beasts on Geonosis.

◆ Brave hunters can earn good money capturing dangerous galactic beasts alive for Geonosian venations.

Claw-tip

The acklay walks on hypertrophied fingertips, which form huge claws used for both locomotion and stabbing attacks. Waving these horrific hatchets wildly, the acklay can cut most beings to pieces without suffering a scratch.

Sensory hairs in hardened exoskeletal claw provide sensation

Piercing claw-tip is horn fused with solid bone

Semi-prehensile tail wraps around branches for stability

Quills erect during combat

Secondary eyes for heat vision

Nexu

Native to Cholganna, the nexu lives and hunts in cool forests. Its secondary eyes see in infrared wavelengths, allowing it to spy the tell-tale heat signatures of warm-blooded prey, especially the arboreal octopi it relishes, but also the stoutly-built bark rats that form the bulk of its diet. The nexu seizes prey in its broad, toothy mouth, then bites and shakes the creature to death. Sharp quills on the nexu's back discourage attack from above.

Fur for insulation in cool environment

Short, secondary claw for gripping treetrunks on home planet

Wide gape

Sprawling stance allows broad footing on leafy canopies

Primary claw for attacking prey

Fleshy and plodding, the reek is nonetheless a strong beast and a powerful fighter. The reek's powerful jaw muscles are built to chop tough wood-moss chunks into pieces, but its bite can nip limbs off even more easily.

Red coloration produced by unnatural meat diet

Central horn for goring opponent (in wild, used in dominance combat with other reek)

Tough skin

Reek

Reek live on the Codian Moon, where small herds are highly territorial over their patches of wood-moss turf. Unfortunately for the herbivorous reek, it was discovered that the beast can be starved into carnivorism to provide excellent entertainment in the arena. Fed on meat alone, the reek will die, but arena specimens are given just enough plant food to keep them hungry and strong.

Horn-teeth grow continuously

Mottling identifies subspecies

Sprawling posture makes reek relatively slow-moving

Cheek horns for dominance-combat headlocks

Front claws for digging wood-moss

Pullback for cutting sweep

Horizontal parry

Jedi in Battle

JEDI KNIGHTS use their powers of subtle perception to resolve conflicts through negotiation and diplomacy. They seek peace through justice, knowing that true harmony can rarely be forced upon a situation. Nonetheless, mystical philosophy has never blinded the Jedi to the practical need for force in intractable situations, and the most studied Jedi diplomats are capable of drawing their lightsabers in an eyeblink when crisis demands it. When war preparations are discovered on Geonosis, Mace Windu is quick to act, leading a Jedi expedition of all available fighters to rescue Obi-Wan Kenobi.

Different tentacles detect specific chemical signatures

Kit Fisto

As an amphibian Nautolan from Glee Anselm, Kit Fisto can live in air or water. His head tentacles are highly sensitive olfactory organs that allow him to precisely detect subconscious pheromonal expressions of emotion. This ability allows him to take instant advantage of an opponent's uncertainty.

Jedi utility belt

Even as a senior Council member, Windu wears standard robes

Jedi tunic allows ease of movement in combat

BULTAR SWAN

Jedi Knight Bultar Swan draws in her opponents by minimizing her physical movements, striking suddenly with a flawless attack that may be highly complex, yet executed in a single blaze of motion.

Power indicator

Electrum finish for Council senior only

Crystal chamber

Handgrip

Jedi boots offer excellent traction

Synthetic leather surcoat

Lightsaber traditionally worn at left

As a senior member of the Jedi Council, Mace Windu built a new lightsaber for himself. Displaying the highest standards of precision, it represents Mace's mature abilities as a Jedi leader.

Mace Windu

A Form VII instructor, Mace Windu is one of the best living lightsaber fighters in the Jedi Order. Only high-level masters of multiple forms can achieve and control Form VII. This dangerous regimen cuts perilously close to the Sith focus on physical combat ability.

Blade projection
plate

Activator

Handgrip
ridges

Blade length
adjust

KIT FISTO'S
LIGHTSABER

Activator
matrix

Blade length
adjust

Radiator
casing segment

BULTAR SWAN'S
LIGHTSABER

JEDI WEAPONS
Every hand-built
lightsaber expresses
the individuality of
its builder, although
there are few
differences in
function.

PLO KOON'S
LIGHTSABER

Shaak Ti

Shaak Ti fights at her best in group combat
as she is biologically adapted for moving in
dense crowds. She darts with
ease through chaotic melees,
where others struggle amidst
the complexity of movements.

Hollow montrals
sense space
ultrasonically

Barriss Offee

The Padawan learner of Luminara
Unduli, Barriss specializes in tandem
fighting. She uses the Force to
harmonize her actions perfectly
with her partner, making for a
pair that is more powerful
than the sum of its parts.

Intense
gaze is
half-inward

Two-handed
grip for
control

Common
lightsaber design

Chalactan
tattoos

Jedi in battle must resist
the temptation to use the
evil power of hate
and anger, even
against Sith enemies.

Headdress conceals
extrasensory organs
sensitive to dryness

Tattoo represents
dedication to
a physical
specialization

Luminara
Unduli

Through many years of
practice, Luminara has
increased her joints'
flexibility to easily allow
extreme lightsaber moves
that are impossible for
ordinary humanoids.

DATA FILE

◆ Special lightsaber
disciplines take advantage
of non-humanoid abilities
such as 360-degree vision.

◆ Jedi train constantly
with their lightsabers,
whether alone on long
field assignments or with
colleagues at the Temple.

Lightsaber Combat

THE LIGHTSABER is a powerful symbol of discipline as well as a weapon. In the hands of the untrained, the lightsaber is worse than useless against modern blasters, and may even injure its user. But in the hands of a Jedi, the lightsaber can become as powerful as any weapon turned against it, deflecting energy bolts back at attackers in a deadly hail and leaving the Jedi wielder untouched. In its highest form, lightsaber combat becomes a subtle and intricate art, but every Jedi begins by learning its first principles.

THE SEVEN FORMS
Seven forms of lightsaber combat have been developed since the foundation of the Jedi Order. Each represents a distinct approach or philosophy, and has its particular strengths. Jedi may specialize in dedication to a particular form or build their own fighting style with elements of multiple forms, although this takes special discipline.

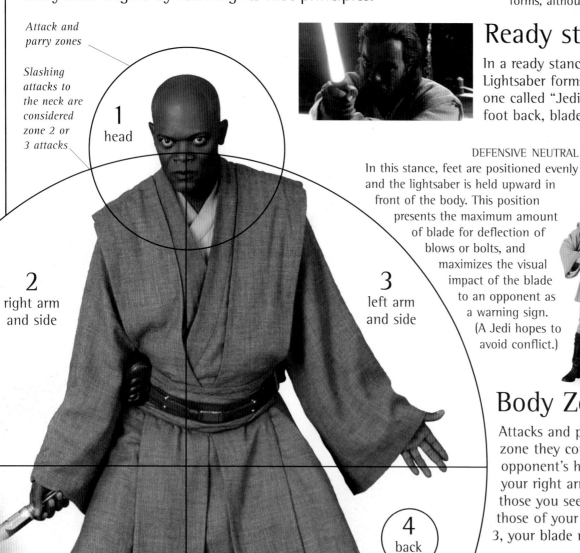

Attack and parry zones

Slashing attacks to the neck are considered zone 2 or 3 attacks

1
head

2
right arm and side

3
left arm and side

4
back

5
right leg

6
left leg

Ready stances

In a ready stance, a Jedi is prepared for combat. Lightsaber forms include many ready stances, but the one called "Jedi ready" is the most common: dominant foot back, blade held in parry position on dominant side.

DEFENSIVE NEUTRAL
In this stance, feet are positioned evenly and the lightsaber is held upward in front of the body. This position presents the maximum amount of blade for deflection of blows or bolts, and maximizes the visual impact of the blade to an opponent as a warning sign. (A Jedi hopes to avoid conflict.)

Blade held toward opponent's eyes

AGGRESSIVE NEUTRAL
In this stance, feet are placed evenly with the point of the blade closest to enemy. It presents the minimum visual blade target for attack and tracking.

Body Zones

Attacks and parries are described in terms of the body zone they concern. "Attack 1" is a blow to the opponent's head, "parry 2" the block of an attack to your right arm or side, and so on. Attack zones are those you see on your opponent, while parry zones are those of your own body. So to go from attack 3 to parry 3, your blade must move from your right side to your left.

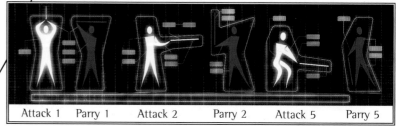

Attack 1	Parry 1	Attack 2	Parry 2	Attack 5	Parry 5

IDEAL FORM
In ideal form, attacks are horizontal side swipes and parries are made with the blade upright, pushing the point of the enemy's blade safely away. This rule is reversed for attack and defense of the head, where the attacker slashes down and the defender holds his blade parallel to the ground.

VELOCITIES

To develop lightning reflexes and tight control, Jedi face each other in drills called velocities. The tenth velocity sequence takes each opponent through a series of attacks and parries and is repeated in turn at ever greater speed until one opponent is felled or yields with the declaration, "Solah!"

| Attack 1/Parry 1 | Attack 6/Parry 6 | Attack 5/Parry 5 | Attack 3/Parry 3 | Attack 2/Parry 2 |

Foundations

Jedi in training run lightsaber velocities endlessly to increase their key skills and physical stamina. Building on these basics, Jedi can go beyond what is physically possible, allowing the Force to flow through them. A Padawan practices for the trials of passage using dulon: Solo sequences of moves in which the opponents are only envisioned. The patterns of velocities and dulon prepare a Jedi for the unpredictable realm of live combat.

Two-handed grip gives best control

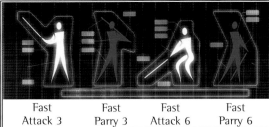

The Sith use synthetic lightsaber crystals, which generate a stronger blade when energized by the dark side of the Force. The advantage is slim, but the very appearance of a red blade is a symbol of hateful power.

Parry 4

Parry 1

| Fast Attack 3 | Fast Parry 3 | Fast Attack 6 | Fast Parry 6 |

LIVE COMBAT FORM

In contrast to ideal form, in live combat, blade attitude for attack is often angled downward to minimize body movement and increase speed. But keeping in mind the ideal distinction between attack and defense attitudes improves precision.

KAI-KAN
Great lightsaber duels have been studied throughout the ages by sword-masters. Kai-kan are dangerous re-enactments of these combats that only well-trained Jedi attempt.

Drop stance

Push-down parry 3

In advanced lightsaber combat, the Force plays a role larger than physical skill alone. Combatants use Force powers for attack and defense, while Sith attempt to break a Jedi's inner spirit.

JEDI MOVES
JUNG: 180-degree turn
JUNG MA: 360-degree spin to gain power for an attack
SAI: Force-assisted jump to evade an attack to the legs
SHUN: One-handed grip, spinning lightsaber 360 degrees to gain speed for an attack

LONDON, NEW YORK, DELHI,
MUNICH and JOHANNESBURG

DORLING KINDERSLEY

SENIOR EDITOR Simon Beecroft
PROJECT ART EDITORS Guy Harvey and Nick Avery
EDITORIAL ASSISTANT Julia March
PUBLISHING MANAGER Cynthia O'Neill Collins
MANAGING ART EDITOR Cathy Tincknell
DTP DESIGNER Jill Bunyan
PRODUCTION Nicola Torode

LUCASFILM

ART EDITOR Iain R. Morris
EDITOR Jonathan W. Rinzler
IMAGE COORDINATOR Aaron Henderson
MANAGER OF IMAGE ARCHIVES Tina Mills

First published in Great Britain in 2002 by
Dorling Kindersley Limited,
80 Strand, London WC2E 0RL

2 4 6 8 10 9 7 5 3 1

A CIP catalogue record for this book is available from the British Library.

ISBN 0-7513-3745-5

Color reproduction by Mullis Morgan Group, England
Printed and bound in Italy by A. Mondadori Editore, Verona

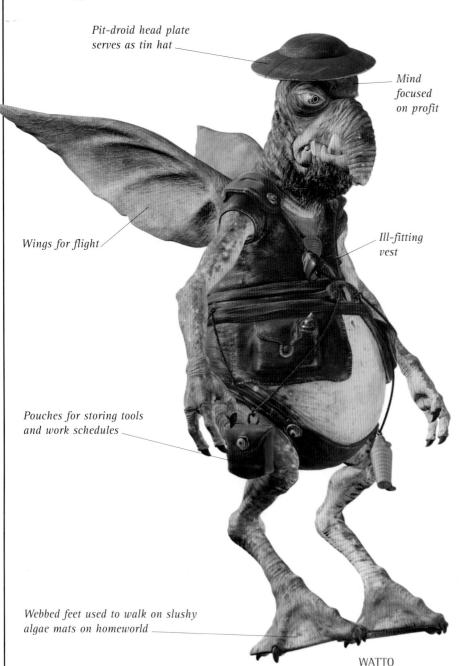

Pit-droid head plate
serves as tin hat

Mind
focused
on profit

Wings for flight

Ill-fitting
vest

Pouches for storing tools
and work schedules

Webbed feet used to walk on slushy
algae mats on homeworld

WATTO

Acknowledgements

A tiger team of authorities and experts behind the scenes contributed greatly to this book with consultation and creative input. It is my pleasure to thank in particular:

Prof. Greg Aldrete of the University of Wisconsin Green Bay, for his work on the role of communication in building the power of an emperor; FBI Special Agent Matt Bliss, for his first-hand information on real-world bounty hunters, military training, and indoctrination approaches; Fencing master and swordsman extraordinaire Jack "Tony" Bobo, Esq., for developing the principles of lightsaber combat. (Whom else could I have called who would already have had his sword lying out and ready?); "Jedi" Steve Drago, for assistance in studying and practicing lightsaber moves; Stunt Coordinator Nick Gillard, high saber-master of the Jedi Temple, for explaining his nuanced work in creating prequel lightsaber combat, and for personally training me on-set in one of his fight

sequences; Prof. Mark Spencer of the University of Colorado, for anthropological consultation on the Tusken Raiders; Designers Iain Morris, Guy Harvey, and Nick Avery, who produced inspiring layouts of bold and aggressive design; DK Editor Simon Beecroft, for his vital organizing influence and his keen and constructive editorial eye; Master photographer Alex Ivanov, who captured the beautiful image of the "unshootable" 90-facet Great Holocron. (As Don Bies has observed, the man truly paints with light); ILM master modelmakers Don Bies and John Goodson, for the precision-crafted Holocrons and the clone trooper rifle cutaway; Lucasfilm master sculptor Robert Barnes, who created creature models for this book that looked real enough to bite us; John Kelly, for digital manipulation on the clone trooper rifle cutaway and artwork for the lightsaber combat sequences; Fyberdyne Laboratories' Ed Endres, whose superb work made it possible for me to explore the experience of wearing full body armor like a clone

trooper; Cynthia O'Neill Collins and Cathy Tincknell at DK for kindly supporting the effort it took to make this project happen.

And as always the team at Lucasfilm: Lucy Autrey Wilson, for encouraging backstory coordination to make this project the best it could be; Jonathan Rinzler for braving new territory with us; Howard Roffman for an enjoyable evening discussion on the nature of Sith evil.

Finally, to my supportive family, particularly my brother Michael Reynolds in whose comfortable home I wrote the last of this text between visits to White Castle and the emergency room.

Dorling Kindersley would also like to thank: Sue Rostoni, Chris Cerasi, Steve Sansweet, Leland Chee, Stacey Cheregotis, and Chris Gollaher, for approvals.